BERTIE AND ALIX

BERTIE AND ALIX

ANATOMY OF A ROYAL MARRIAGE

Graham and Heather Fisher

ROBERT HALE & COMPANY · LONDON

© *Graham and Heather Fisher Ltd 1974*
First published in Great Britain 1974

ISBN 0 7091 4477 6

Robert Hale & Company
63 Old Brompton Road
London SW7

MADE AND PRINTED IN GREAT BRITAIN BY
THE GARDEN CITY PRESS LIMITED
LETCHWORTH, HERTFORDSHIRE SG6 1JS

CONTENTS

ILLUSTRATIONS

The above illustrations numbered 1, 2, 7, 12, 18, 19, and 22, are reproduced from the Mansell Collection; illustration number 4 was supplied by Paul Popper Limited; all the remaining photographs are reproduced from the Radio Times Hulton Picture Library.

AUTHORS' FOREWORD

This is the story of the Queen's great-grandparents, King Edward VII and Queen Alexandra, and their married life together . . . how their marriage was carefully arranged after the royal fashion of the time and how, for better or worse, it worked out.

Except as far as is necessary to paint the back-cloth against which they moved, we have made no attempt to deal with constitutional or political matters. Nor have we made any attempt to assess Edward VII as either monarch or statesman.

Our concern has been to show what Bertie—as the family called him—was like in his personal life . . . as a man, a husband, a father and a lusty lover; to show what Alix was like as a woman, a wife and a mother.

We are grateful to the Librarian and staff of the London Library and to Miss Barrett and others in Bromley Central Library for their patience and help during the long period we were researching this book.

We intend it to entertain as much as instruct. Nevertheless, we have adhered strictly to the known facts. Where dialogue is used, the words are what the people concerned were heard to say or what they themselves recorded (in their letters, journals or memoirs) had been said.

G. and H.F.

Keston Park,
Kent

For
JAMES and ROBERT
(when they are older)

PRINCIPAL CHARACTERS

The Husband:
Bertie   Queen Victoria's eldest son, Albert Edward, Prince of Wales, later King Edward VII.

The Wife:
Alix   Alexandra Caroline Marie Charlotte Louise Julia, Princess of Denmark, Princess of Wales, later Queen Alexandra.

The children, and their families:
Eddy   Albert Victor, Duke of Clarence.
Georgie   George, Duke of York, Prince of Wales, later King George V.
May   Georgie's wife, Princess Victoria Mary of Teck, later Queen Mary.
David   Georgie's eldest son, later King Edward VIII and Duke of Windsor.
Bertie   Georgie's son, Albert, Duke of York, later King George VI.
       (Georgie and May had four other children: Mary, Princess Royal; Henry, Duke of Gloucester; George, Duke of Kent; and Prince John.)
Louise   Princess Royal and Duchess of Fife.
MacDuff   Louise's husband, the Duke of Fife.
Toria   Princess Victoria (who never married).
Harry   Princess Maud, later Queen Maud of Norway.
Charles   Maud's husband, Prince Charles of Denmark, later King Haakon VII of Norway.

Bertie's parents:
Mama (or Gan-gan)   Queen Victoria.
Papa   Albert, Prince Consort.

Alix's parents:

Apapa
: Prince Christian of Schleswig-Holstein-Sonder-burg-Glucksburg, later King Christian IX of Denmark.

Amama
: Princess Louise of Hesse-Cassel, later Queen of Denmark.

Bertie's brothers and sisters and their families:

Vicky
: Victoria, Princess Royal, Crown Princess of Prussia, Empress of Germany.

Fritz
: Vicky's husband, Crown Prince Frederick William, later Emperor Frederick III.

Willy
: Vicky's son, later Kaiser William II.

Alice
: Princess Louis of Hesse.

Louis
: Alice's husband, the Grand Duke of Hesse-Darmstadt.

Alicky (or Alix)
: Alice's daughter, Alexandra, later Empress of Russia.

Nicky
: Alicky's husband, the Tsarevitch Nicholas, later Tsar Nicholas II.

Affie
: Alfred, Duke of Edinburgh (married the Grand Duchess Marie, only daughter of Tsar Alexander II).

Lenchen
: Princess Helena (married Prince Christian of Schleswig-Holstein).

Louise
: Princess Louise (married the Duke of Argyll).

Arthur
: Arthur, Duke of Connaught (married Princess Louise of Prussia).

Leo
: Leopold, Duke of Albany (married Princess Helen of Waldeck Pyrmont).

Baby
: Princess Beatrice (married Prince Henry of Battenberg).

Alix's brothers and sisters and their families:

Freddy
: Later King Frederick VIII of Denmark.

Willy
: Later King George I of the Hellenes.

Olga
: Willy's wife and niece of Tsar Alexander II.

Minnie
: Princess Marie Sophia Frederika Dagmar, later Marie Fedorovna, Empress of Russia.

Sasha
: Minnie's husband, Tsar Alexander III.

Nicky
: Minnie's son, Nicholas (who married Alice's daughter, Alicky).

Thyra
: Married Ernest Augustus, Duke of Cumberland.

Waldemar
: Married Marie, daughter of the Duc de Chartres.

PART ONE

A Marriage has been Arranged

A BRIDE FOR BERTIE

Queen Victoria's sitting room in Windsor Castle was crammed with furniture; cluttered with bric-à-brac; festooned with portraits . . . so many portraits that the crimson flock on the walls was almost hidden by the multitude of gilt frames.

To the left of the large gilt-framed mirror above the mantlepiece hung the family group—the Queen, the Prince Consort and their elder children—which Landseer had painted when the children were small. Across the room, but reflected in the mirror so that it seemed to hang beside Landseer's family group, a portrait of the Prince Consort—Victoria's beloved Albert—looked down at the Queen as she sat at her writing table.

Mantelpiece, side cabinets and the drum-shaped table behind the Queen were all crowded with bric-à-brac . . . clocks and busts, vases and photographs, toby jugs and china cats, among them a small statuette of the Queen on horseback. She had been very young, fresh to the throne, when that statuette was fashioned.

She was thirty-eight now, and nearly twenty years of monarchy and the births of nine children had combined to make her look older than her years.

Her first child, Vicky, had been born within ten months of marriage. The last, Baby, had arrived only the previous April, less than a year before Vicky, seventeen now, had married the tall, floridly-moustached Prince Frederick of Prussia—Fritz, as the Queen affectionately called him.

The Queen drew a sheet of her personal notepaper, decorated with a small woodcut of Windsor Castle, towards her with chubby fingers. She wrote the date on it: 31st March 1858.

She was writing to Vicky in Berlin as she had done every week, and sometimes twice a week, since Vicky and Fritz had been married in the Chapel Royal in January . . . and as she was to continue to do for the next forty years.

"Dearest Child," she began in her fast, sometimes almost illegible handwriting.

Vicky, oldest of the royal children, was the Prince Consort's favourite. The Queen herself had no particular favourite, though there was perhaps an extra soft spot in her heart for Baby, the youngest.

But if the Queen had no favourite among her children, she knew very well who was not her favourite—Bertie, second of her children and oldest of her sons, the sixteen-year-old Prince of Wales.

When Bertie was born his mother's hope had been that he would grow up to be like his father, that most perfect (as she thought) of human beings. But more and more it dawned upon her that Bertie was not, and never would be, like his father. Even the combined efforts of Albert and his confidential adviser, Baron Stockmar, had proved quite unable to bring about the desired transformation. Tutors recommended by Stockmar had taught him English, Latin, French and German (with the emphasis on German so that Bertie, all his life, was to speak with a guttural r). He had been taught writing and calculation, geography and chemistry, drawing, music and the Scriptures. He had been taught gymnastics and military science; dancing and riding. He had been shown how to shoot and fish, hunt and stalk. All, it seemed to his mother, to little avail. The reports she had of him showed him to be still undisciplined and selfish. His temper was bad . . . and getting worse . . . though it was encouraging to learn from Dr Combe, the phrenologist, that Bertie's moral and intellectual bumps were enlarging, promising an improvement in his powers of control.

In his mother's view, Bertie was idle, lazy, ignorant and dull; interested, it seemed, in nothing but clothes. Inclined to over-indulge to an extent which sometimes induced a sick headache. And still fresh in the Queen's mind was that business at Konigswinter the previous July. He had been sent there to study and on the very first evening, after dining too well, he had caught hold of the nearest pretty girl and promptly proceeded to kiss her. He had been suitably admonished, of course.

It would be a good thing, the Queen thought, when Bertie was old enough to marry and settle down. What he needed, more than anything, was the right sort of wife to keep him straight.

"We must look out for princesses for Bertie," the Queen wrote to Vicky in that letter from Windsor in March 1858. "Oh, if you could find us one!"

She proceeded to detail the necessary qualifications. A suitable wife would have to be a year or two younger than Bertie . . . "therefore fourteen or fifteen now". She would need to be "pretty, quiet and clever and sensible".

It was the first of many letters in which the Queen was to touch on the subject. In another letter, shortly afterwards, she laid down further qualifications: "Good looks, education, character, intellect and disposition."

Vicky, a bright, intelligent, romantically-minded young woman, was only too eager to play matchmaker to her brother. From her vantage point in the pale pink Neue Palais she began to make discreet inquiries concerning Europe's available princesses. The first two names suggested by Mama—Princess Anna of Hesse and Princess Elizabeth of Wied—did not strike her as at all suitable.

Elizabeth, she reported back, was "not graceful" and did "not look very ladylike". She had a long chin and her nose was not pretty. "Certainly the opposite to Bertie's usual taste," she added, knowing her brother.

Anna was no better. According to Vicky, she had "an incipient twitching in her eyes" and "her teeth are nearly all spoilt". Those twitching eyes, she added, were also small and insignificant. To make matters worse, Anna had a deep, gruff voice and a rather abrupt way of speaking.

Over the next eighteen months, in her once-weekly, sometimes twice-weekly, letters from Windsor Castle, Balmoral Castle and Osborne House on the Isle of Wight to Vicky in Berlin, Queen Victoria diligently pursued the question of a bride for Bertie.

Of all this, of course, Bertie knew nothing. In accordance with his parents' determined resolve to make him more like his father, he was sent to Rome, with an increased allowance of five hundred pounds a year, to study art and archeology; to Holyroodhouse for a three-months' cram course designed to make good any deficiencies in his already extensive education; and then to Oxford with strict instructions from Papa that he

was not to slouch, lounge about or go around with his hands in
his pockets. He was to lodge in a house in the town so that he did
not mix too freely with any of the other, less regal, undergraduates and he would, of course, have his own chef. He was
not to play cards or billiards, cricket or football, though the
occasional game of real tennis (lawn tennis did not yet exist)
could perhaps be permitted. He was also gazetted a lieutenant-
colonel, but that was as far as his father was prepared to go
towards satisfying his craving for a military career.

The spring of 1859 brought a brief break in the interchange of
letters between Queen Victoria and her eldest daughter . . . but
only because there was, for a few weeks, no need of them. The
birth of Vicky's first child, Willy, had made Queen Victoria a
grandmother. It had been a difficult, painful birth and almost the
first thing Vicky did when she was up and about again was
return to England to visit her parents. Now mother and daughter
could talk face to face on the all-important subject of a bride for
Bertie. Prince Albert, too, joined in the family discussions on the
point, and Vicky returned to Berlin to renew her inquiries and
redouble her efforts while Queen Victoria, by letter, continued
to bombard her with names and suggestions.

What about Princess Marie of Hohenzollern?

"Quite lovely", Vicky wrote back. But Marie, she added, was
a Catholic. So Marie of Hohenzollern was promptly deleted
from the Queen's list of eligible princesses.

If not Marie, then how about the Princess of Dessau? Too old
for Bertie, Vicky informed Mama.

The Weimar princesses, then? Both delicate and not pretty.

The Princess of Sweden? Much too young.

Princess Marie of the Netherlands? Too plain for Bertie.

Princess Alexandrine of Prussia? Neither pretty nor clever.

The Princess of Meiningen? Queen Victoria deleted that name
herself. Bertie had met the Meiningen princess and promptly said
that he did not like her.

Was there not a young Princess of Altenburg? If there was,
Vicky knew nothing about her.

A degree of frustration was beginning to creep into the
matchmaking correspondence between mother and daughter.

"God knows where the young lady we want is to be found,"
the Queen wrote, despairingly.

"There is a great dearth of nice princesses at present," Vicky reminded her.

"Tax your brain," the Queen urged.

Vicky did. She sat for hours turning the pages of the *Almanach de Gotha* in the hope of stumbling across some fresh name. She had no success.

"The difficulties are so very, very great to find the person wanted," she lamented to Mama.

BEWITCHING PRINCESS

The dinner party which Queen Victoria and the Prince Consort gave at Windsor on 9th November 1860 was hardly the gayest of occasions. The Queen spoke little, concentrating on her food, which she was inclined to gobble. Out of deference to her, conversation around the rest of the table was mainly in whispers, with guests kept busy preventing the servants from whipping their plates away before they had finished.

The party had been planned as a celebration for Bertie's nineteenth birthday. But Bertie himself was not there. The ship bringing him back from a tour of Canada and the United States, tightly sandwiched between his terms at Oxford, was overdue.

The Queen and her stiff, reserved husband sat side by side at the dinner table. On Albert's other side sat young Mrs Augustus Paget, the former Countess Hohenthal. Newly married to the British minister to Denmark, she was in England on her honeymoon.

Wally, as she was known to the Royal Family, knew all about the intensive and, so far, fruitless search to find a suitable bride for the Prince of Wales, a princess who would be at one and the same time attractive enough to appeal to him and strong enough in character to keep him straight. As Vicky's lady-in-waiting, she had helped diligently with the inquiries into the different names so far suggested by Queen Victoria.

Now, over dinner, she suggested a name which Queen Victoria had so far ignored—Princess Alix of Denmark.

"Have you met her?" asked the Prince Consort.

Young Mrs Paget had not. But she had heard a great deal about her from her husband.

"And what does Mr Paget think of her?"

"That she is the most charming, pretty and delightful young princess it is possible to imagine."

The Prince Consort turned towards his wife and repeated what Wally had told him.

It was not the first time the name of Princess Alix had cropped up since the Queen first started looking round for a wife for her eldest son. Uncle Leopold had included it in a list of possible princesses he had compiled and sent over from Belgium. *The Times* had mentioned it the previous July, along with the names of six other princesses, all of whom had already been investigated and found wanting. That Princess Alix had not yet been similarly investigated was due to the fact that the Queen wanted no trouble with her relatives in Germany. Alix's father, Prince Christian of Schleswig-Holstein-Sonderburg-Glucksburg, was heir to the throne of Denmark and everyone knew that sooner or later there was going to be trouble between Germany and Denmark over the disputed duchies of Schleswig and Holstein. For Bertie to marry Alix—even if she proved suitable in all other respects—would certainly not please Germany. And there were other reasons. Alix's family, in the Queen's view, was not of good stock, bad on the mother's side, foolish on the father's.

Yet she must find a bride for Bertie somewhere. He was nineteen now and, despite all her efforts, she was no nearer finding someone suitable than she had been when he was sixteen.

Dinner over, the Queen beckoned Wally to her.

"When you return to Denmark," she said, confidentially, "be so good as to send me all the information you can get about Princess Alix. A photograph also."

But all this, she was quick to impress upon the young newlywed, must be accomplished without arousing the slightest suspicion in the minds of Alix's parents, Prince Christian and Princess Louise.

The Pagets returned to Copenhagen the following month, a bitterly cold December with the sea around the Danish capital frozen solid. So cold was it that it was a full ten days before young Mrs Paget ventured out. When she did, she did not go straight to Alix's parents. That would only have aroused the very suspicions Queen Victoria was most anxious to avoid. Instead, as wife of the British minister, she made a series of duty calls on other members of the Danish royal family, among them the imperiously handsome Queen Dowager. That way, it seemed natural enough that she should call in turn upon Princess Louise at the Yellow Palace on the Amaliegade, an unpretentious, even slightly shabby, royal residence looking more like an hotel than a royal palace.

Princess Louise—"a very pretty woman with fine eyes and a nice figure"—welcomed her warmly. Caught up as she was in the spirit of romantic intrigue, Wally Paget, though only twenty-one, was yet cautious enough not to plunge straight into the real purpose of her visit.

She and Princess Louise talked awhile of this and that. Alix's father, a tall, fair-haired, amiable man, drifted into the room and joined briefly in the conversation.

A turn in the conversation gave Wally the opportunity she was seeking.

"My husband has spoken to me so often about Princess Alix," she said. "I hoped I might be permitted to see her."

Alix was sent for.

She was just turned sixteen that December day, having celebrated her birthday on the first of the month. Tall for her age. She was a natural, unassuming girl who hardly ever thought of herself as Princess Alexandra Caroline Marie Charlotte Louise Julia, the somewhat cumbersome mouthful bestowed upon her at birth. She thought of herself, as her family and friends did, simply as Alix.

A pretty girl, though not yet the elegant beauty she was to become later. Rather thin-faced with a long, thin, aristocratic nose; serious in repose but with features which became light and bright when she gave way, as she did often, to smiles or husky laughter. She had large blue eyes, Wally noted, and a good complexion. Her brown hair hung down about her shoulders in long, soft ringlets.

She was, at the time, a somewhat shy girl. Unpunctual, as she was to be all her life, with no idea of time. Child-like, even childish at times, as she was also to be all her life. Unspoilt.

There was little danger of any of Prince Christian's children being spoilt. Until he found himself, suddenly and unexpectedly, heir to the throne of Denmark, there had been little money for even the smallest of childhood luxuries and early on both Alix and Minnie—the family's pet name for her younger sister, dark-eyed and dark-haired, less pretty but more vivacious—had had to learn to make their own dresses and knit their own stockings.

By princely standards, Prince Christian had long been a poor man, owing almost everything he possessed—his home in the Yellow Palace, his commission as a captain in the Royal Horse Guards and his small private income—to his wife's uncle, King Christian VIII. With the King's death, the accession of the excessively fat, twice-divorced and childless Frederick VII, and his own nomination as Frederick's heir, his income had risen from £800 to £2000 a year. Her parents might now be able to buy Alix a new dress when the party season came round, but she still had to take it off and put it neatly away as soon as she returned home; still had to help out, as did her brothers and sisters, when visitors came to stay.

Alix may not have seen the Yellow Palace, her childhood home, as shabby on the outside and barely furnished on the inside. But that was how it appeared to those same visitors. Certainly she never thought of her father as Denmark's future king. She saw him instead as a kind, rather easy-going parent who taught her and the other children to ride and skate, showed them how to do handstands and cartwheels in the palace court-yard, and took them for walks to see the shipping in the harbour. Her mother, she sensed, was the more dominant of her parents, a clever, intelligent woman who taught her children German and music. Their nanny taught them English and there was a governess for French. This, apart from politeness and good manners, was the limit of their education.

Wally said her goodbyes and hurried off, but not before she had contrived to borrow a photograph of Alix from the girl's mother . . . without arousing undue suspicion, she hoped.

Post-haste she sent the photograph to Vicky in Berlin. Vicky, she knew, would pass on both the photograph and her comments about Alix to Mama in England.

Vicky did. "Just the style Bertie admires," she wrote as a caption.

Queen Victoria showed the photograph to her husband.

"From that photograph, I would marry her myself at once," commented Albert, not a man given to quips.

"What a pity she is who she is," sighed the Queen, and she

made a mental note not to let Bertie see the photograph . . . at least, not yet . . . not until she herself had made up her mind about Alix.

Once again the Queen seated herself at her writing table and penned another long, detailed letter to Vicky in Berlin. She wanted every possible scrap of information about Alix that Vicky could obtain, she wrote.

Vicky, in turn, wrote again to Wally in Copenhagen. Back came a reply assuring her that Alix had a "gentle and ladylike manner and a sweet voice and expression". The Danish princess was not unlike Vicky's own sister, Princess Alice, Wally Paget added to underline and emphasize what she had already written.

All this information Vicky sent back to Mama, with the added comment: "That sounds very inviting, does it not?"

Indeed, it did, Queen Victoria was no longer quite so concerned about the almost inevitable reaction to be expected from her German relatives if her eldest son married the Danish princess. But she had fresh doubts of another sort. All this talk of gentle, ladylike sweetness was all very well, but it would take more than that to attract Bertie in the first place and keep him straight after marriage.

"Excessive gentleness," she propounded to Vicky in yet another letter, "unless coupled with great cleverness and firmness, would not do . . . Superiority of mind and a certain determination are very necessary—else advantage is taken and rudeness and an amount of tyrannizing people takes place."

As future events were to show, the Queen knew her eldest son only too well.

"You will understand me," she wrote. "Those who never knock under but hold their own are always those most liked and who get on best with the nameless individual."

And she still wanted to know a great deal more about Alix. What sort of education had she had? What was her general character like? Was she clever, quiet, not frivolous or vain? Queen Victoria was nothing if not thorough.

Then, out of the blue, came a letter from Wally in Copenhagen which was like a bombshell to both Vicky and her mother. There was a rumour going round, she wrote to Vicky, that the son of Tsar Alexander II was about to ask for the hand of Princess Alix. Vicky passed the news on to Mama.

"It would be dreadful if this pearl went to the horrid Russians . . . Princesses do not spring up like mushrooms out of the earth or grow upon trees."

Queen Victoria, receiving her daughter's letter, became equally alarmed. If she lost Alix, who else was there for Bertie? The time for dilly-dallying was clearly past. Now it was time for action. Some member of her own family must take a good look at Princess Alix so that a final decision could be made. And Alix's parents must be given an inkling of what was in the Queen's mind. All most discreetly, of course.

The path of discretion lay, as previously, through Vicky in Berlin and Wally in Copenhagen. Queen Victoria wrote again to Vicky and Vicky to Wally. Wally wrote back suggesting that Alix could perhaps come to England. Then the queen could see her for herself.

To Vicky, it was a much too straightforward suggestion. "Too great a step for the beginning," she wrote back in alarm. How about Strelitz?

Strelitz was the home of the Grand Duchess Augusta of Mecklenburg-Strelitz, who was related to both Queen Victoria and Alix's mother. What more natural than that Victoria's daughter, Vicky, and Louise's daughter, Alix, should visit the same relative at the same time.

Wally was deputed to see Alix's mother again; to ask her if her elder daughter was likely to be visiting Germany in the near future and to say that, if so, Queen Victoria's eldest daughter would welcome the opportunity of meeting her. She was also to ask Princess Louise for some more photographs of her daughter. A clever mother, Vicky reasoned, would know what to read into all that. And in case Princess Louise was not quite clever enough, "I should have no objection to you compromising me slightly . . . and if you were a little indiscreet," Vicky informed Wally. "I wish Princess Christian to read my thoughts between the lines, so do not be too timid."

Alix's mother, as it turned out, needed few hints and very little prompting. But time was slipping away and telegrams now took the place of letters.

Could Alix be there between 13th May and 8th June? She could. Vicky, in turn, arranged to visit the Grand Duchess on 29th May.

Alix herself, when the time came for her to visit the sometimes sharply-spoken Grand Duchess, still had no inkling of what was afoot. She was, in consequence, neither excited nor nervous, but simply her natural, unassuming self. Vicky, her green eyes studying the younger girl intently, was immediately taken with her.

Skilfully, as they walked together among the statues in the formal garden, Vicky plied Alix with questions. What plays had she seen? What music did she like best? Who were her favourite painters?

To all her questions Alix replied simply and honestly, with not the slightest idea that she was being subtly cross-examined and assessed, that every word and gesture was being carefully memorized for the benefit of Queen Victoria.

Vicky could hardly wait to dash off her latest report to Mama of all Alix had said ("she speaks English and German without the slightest accent") and done ("her walk, manner and carriage are perfect"), of how she looked ("a lovely figure, but very thin, a complexion as beautiful as possible") and how she had behaved ("as simple and natural and unaffected as possible").

She wrote quickly, enthusiastically, her letter loaded with superlatives: "I never set eyes on a sweeter creature . . . one of the most ladylike and aristocratic people I ever saw . . . bewitching."

She was, if anything, inclined to let her enthusiasm run away with her. Alix did not speak English "without the slightest accent". Not then; not ever. But, as Queen Victoria well knew, her eldest daughter was sometimes inclined to exaggerate the good qualities of people she liked, and the Queen made allowance for that. But a note from Fritz which Vicky enclosed with her own letter removed any lingering doubt the Queen may have had. Her son-in-law, too, was completely enthused about Alix, and Fritz—like Bertie—was not a person easily enthused.

If there was any slight doubt still in the Queen's mind, it was that Alix was too good for Bertie. "May he only be worthy of such a jewel," she wrote to Vicky.

It remained now to gauge Bertie's own reaction to the idea of marrying Alix. Difficult and quick-tempered as he could be, he was not, as his mother knew, a young man to be pushed into marriage against his will. She left it to his father to sound him out.

Bertie seemed hesitant.

"These days," he told his father, "if a person rashly proposes and then repents, the relations—if not the lady herself—do not let him off so easily."

He had finished his stint at Oxford and transferred to Cambridge in pursuit of the intensive, all-embracing plan conceived for his education. But he was still permitted to have little contact with other undergraduates. He lived at Madingley Hall, some four miles out and rode to his lectures each day on horseback. But in one thing at least he was beginning to get his own way . . . or, rather, a compromise, which was as much as he could hope for. While still refusing to let him adopt the army as a career, his parents agreed that he could take a ten-week course of training with the Grenadier Guards.

His father, when they next met, again raised the subject of marriage. Bertie was shown photographs of Alix and the letters Vicky and Fritz had written after meeting her at Strelitz.

He would like to meet her, he said.

A further series of letters winged their way back and forth along the two sides of the triangle which linked Queen Victoria with Vicky in Berlin and, through her, with Wally and Alix's mother in Copenhagen. In the arrangements which followed, the spell of military training Bertie had been promised coincidentally came in useful. What would seem more natural than for the Prince of Wales to follow up his spell with the Grenadiers with a trip to Germany to watch army manoeuvres there. Naturally, he would stay with Vicky and Fritz. Naturally, he would go sight-seeing with them. If Alix and her parents chanced to be in Germany at the same time, if they chanced to go sightseeing to the same spot . . . why, then, the two young people could hardly help bumping into each other.

INTERLUDE IN IRELAND

Bertie, as he drilled his squad of Grenadiers on the Curragh, that vast, windswept plain in County Kildare, uttering commands with a guttural inflection which was not always clearly understood, was a rather unhappy and discontented young man. He had long wanted to join the army. Uniforms, martial music . . .

these things appealed to him strongly. But now that he had finally been given his way, things were not working out as he had visualized. That they were not was largely due to the fact that his father, Prince Albert, had promptly worked out one of his grandiose and intensive schemes designed to make a better man of his eldest son. Bertie, he ordained, must learn the duties of every military grade from ensign upwards. He must work diligently enough to gain promotion every two weeks. By the end of ten weeks he could be in command of a battalion. It would, of course, require "some exertion", his father conceded.

For Bertie, it was a quite impossible task. By the end of his first four weeks in camp he was already aware that he had no hope of commanding a battalion by the end of his training. Indeed, the day his parents visited the camp to see how things were coming along, he was not even allowed to command a company. His drill was not up to it, his commanding officer had said, and his commands were indistinct. So on the day of his parents' visit, though wearing the uniform of a staff colonel, he was permitted to perform only the duties of a mere subaltern.

As a result of all this, Bertie was not enjoying army life as much as he had visualized. Still, there were compensations. There was talk of buying him a country estate of his own out of the accumulated revenues of the Duchy of Cornwall. A place in Norfolk had been suggested . . . Sandringham. And once he had finished on the Curragh he would be off to Germany to meet the Danish princess it was suggested he should marry.

Alix still knew nothing of the proposed meeting with Bertie when she left Copenhagen that summer with her parents and the other children for Rumpenheim, the white-fronted, green-shuttered *schloss* of the Hesse-Cassel family, which stood with its dominating clock tower on the wooded banks of the Main near Frankfurt.

Every year, or nearly every year, Princess Louise took her family to spend part of the summer at Rumpenheim. Once it had belonged to her grandfather, Landgrave Frederick. He had bequeathed it to his children on condition that it was used as a holiday home by the whole family in summer. Of his six children, only the beetle-browed Duchess of Cambridge, Augusta of Hesse-Cassel before her marriage to Queen Victoria's uncle, now survived. But the family tradition continued.

Each summer, from far and near, the descendants of Landgrave Frederick came to the eighteenth-century *schloss* . . . sometimes as many as twenty or thirty of them, to say nothing of their servants, until the place threatened almost to burst at the seams. With so many close relatives gathered so closely together, there was inevitably a great deal of good-natured bantering and sometimes a degree of teasing that was not always quite so good-natured . . . such as that which Alix's mother was forced to endure this summer of 1861.

From the moment the Danish family arrived at Rumpenheim, Princess Louise was soundly teased about the possibility that her daughter might marry the Prince of Wales. The Dowager Duchess of Cambridge and her daughter, the Grand Duchess Augusta, went on and on about it.

"I know all," Augusta said, archly, on one occasion.

"I'm very glad that you do," Alix's mother replied. "As for myself, I know nothing."

"If anything comes of it, don't forget that I arranged it in the first place," Augusta crowed.

By now, Princess Louise was quite out of patience with both Augusta and her mother. How like Augusta to try to claim the credit, she thought, when she was really quite opposed to the idea that Alix might marry the Prince of Wales. She was jealous, of course.

Alix was seventeen now, still perhaps more of a girl than a woman; not yet too old to join the younger children in their games in the courtyard; certainly too young to have any say in who she should marry. Others would decide that for her. The Prince of Wales, of course, if he would have her. Failing him, the Tsarevitch of Russia.

While her Hesse-Cassel relatives at Rumpenheim were teasing Louise about her daughter, Bertie in Ireland was beginning to enjoy military life a bit more. He might not hope to command a battalion, but there were always plenty of social diversions. Twice a week he dined in the regimental mess. Twice a week he gave a dinner party for the senior officers. Once a week he was guest-of-honour at dinners given by the other regiments.

These regimental guest nights were always convivial, sometimes boisterous, noisy with masculine banter which sometimes gave way to horseplay as the evening progressed. And it was on one of these nights that it occurred to some of Bertie's fellow-officers that it was high time that someone . . . some girl . . . made a man of the nineteen-year-old Prince of Wales.

Charles Carrington, who had known Bertie at Cambridge, put the idea to a girl called Nellie Clifden. She called herself an actress, but was perhaps more familiar with London's Burlington Arcade, a well known pick-up place of the time, than with the stage of any theatre. She thought it a great lark.

So that night, after lights out, Nellie was smuggled secretly into the quarters of the General Officer Commanding which had been placed at Bertie's disposal out of deference to his princely status. It was Bertie's first experience of sexual pleasure.

"I DO NOT ENVY HIS FUTURE WIFE"

Alix and her sister, Minnie, were going with their parents to visit the cathedral at Speyer, an ancient city of clustered belfreys on the banks of the Rhine. Alix, as she dressed for the journey, had no idea that it was to be a day which would determine the whole course of her life. To her, it was just such a family outing as she had enjoyed with her parents often enough in the past. She wondered which dress to wear. They were going by train, so surely one of her old dresses would be good enough.

No, said her mother decisively, she should wear her new best dress. Alix did as her mother told her and it was in the new dress, walking with her parents, that she entered the cathedral at Speyer. It was 24th September 1861.

At almost the same moment that Alix and her parents were entering the cathedral by one door, another small group of visitors was entering it by another. There were three of them . . . Vicky; her husband, Fritz; and her brother, Bertie. To Vicky's dismay, the Bishop of Speyer recognized her and her husband as they were entering and hurried over to act as their guide.

Step by echoing step, the two groups of seemingly chance visitors, moved towards each other through the vastness of the cathedral. In front of the altar of St Bernard they met and exchanged polite greetings.

Vicky introduced her brother, the Prince of Wales. A usually confident young woman, she felt, for once, "very nervous", she

confessed later. Alix felt shy, but forced herself to overcome her
shyness and make conversation.

Bertie's dark blue eyes studied her intently, but without too
much enthusiasm. Her nose was "too long" and her forehead
"too low", he thought.

At nineteen, rising twenty, he himself had not yet fully
realized the handsomeness which was to come briefly later ...
until good living and dissipation turned him podgy and lethar-
gic. His as yet beardless face, with the "pretty little mouth"
Mama had raved over when he was a baby, was still boyish and
immature for all that Nellie Clifden had recently made a man of
him. To Alix, at first glance, he looked perhaps not unlike
pictures she had seen of his father, the Prince Consort. But the
protuberant eyes and receding chin were inherited from his
mother's side of the family.

The Bishop of Speyer was clearly an encumbrance to the
situation. With the skill of a true match-maker, Vicky deftly
detached him from the main party and led him away. There
were some frescoes she would like him to tell her about, she said.

Later she managed a brief, confidential conversation with
Alix's mother, though what they said to each other was somewhat handicapped by Princess Louise's deafness.

Bertie was glad of this opportunity to become acquainted with
Alix and her family, Vicky remarked.

Yes, the meeting should make things very much easier, Louise
agreed.

"I perceive that the Prince of Wales is not entirely indifferent
to Alix," she continued, "but then he has probably seen few
young princesses and may yet see others who please him
better."

Her remarks gave Vicky a chance to say some of those things
which had to be said ... things which Queen Victoria had made
very clear in her recent letters.

If Bertie should prove to be serious, she asked, would Alix be
permitted to go to England for a time to be with Queen
Victoria.

"Oh, yes, to be sure," Louise replied.

Now for the most important point of all. And the most
delicate. The marriage, if it came about, must not be regarded as
a political alliance. Bertie would be marrying Alix, but England

Bertie and Alix—
Edward Prince of
Wales and
Princess
Alexandra of
Denmark shortly
before their
marriage

The guests assemble at Windsor on the eve of the wedding: (*left to right*) Prince Christian of Denmark, Princess Christian of Denmark (Louise of Hesse-Cassel), Prince Frederick of Denmark, the Crown Prince of Prussia, Princess Louis of Hesse Darmstadt (Princess Alice), Prince Louis of Hesse Darmstadt, Princess Helena, Alix, Bertie, the Crown Princess of Prussia (Princess Victoria), Prince William of Denmark, Princess Dagmar and Princess Louise would not be marrying Denmark. On this point, Queen Victoria, her German relatives in mind, was insistent.

Vicky found things easier than she may have anticipated. It was Alix's mother who raised this delicate point first.

"If something did come of this, it would not be political, thank God, but personal," she said (or so Vicky was to assure Mama).

To hardly anyone's surprise, the two parties found that they were both going on to Heidelberg. They had, it seemed, all booked rooms in the same hotel, Bertie's group in the name of Berg and Alix's parents in that of Holk.

In Heidelberg, Bertie and Alix again saw each other briefly the following day and before parting they exchanged photographs.

With Alix's photograph in his pocket, Bertie travelled back to England to see his parents. His father's first impression was that the two young people had taken "a warm liking" to one another and he was delighted that things seemed to be working out so well. Queen Victoria was not so sure.

Bertie was "well pleased" with Alix, she confided to Vicky. But she was not sure that he was in love. "I don't think he can be," she wrote, "or that he is capable of enthusiasm about anything in the world."

Vicky was disappointed. It gave her a feeling of great sadness, she wrote back, when she thought of Alix—"that sweet lovely flower . . . which would make most men fire and flame"— having so little effect upon Bertie.

"If she fails to kindle a flame, none will ever succeed in doing so." She loved her brother with all her heart and soul, Vicky wrote before adding this telling phrase: "I do not envy his future wife."

Her mother agreed with her. "What you say about Bertie and that lovely young princess is so true—so sad and the prospect a melancholy one."

Bertie, in fact, at this stage of his young life, was in a confused and unhappy state of mind. Naïve as he still was in so many ways, he was almost terrified of the possible consequences of his night of love with Nellie Clifden. His mother, shrewd and observant as she was, knew that something was wrong, though she had no idea what. It seemed to her that he was turning more and more not only against the idea of marrying Alix, but against

marrying anyone at all. It was, she felt, as though he had
suddenly developed some strange fear of marrying and having
children . . ." so strange a fear for so young a man," as she put it.

A LETTER FROM BARON STOCKMAR

A look of shocked disbelief settled upon the normally bland
features of Bertie's father as he read the letter he had just received
from Baron Stockmar in Coburg. As he read on, the reason for
his son's prevarication in the matter of marriage became increasingly clear.

The idea of Nellie Clifden making a man of the young Prince
of Wales was too good a joke for anyone to keep to themselves.
Nellie least of all. She had done her share of boasting since.
Others, too, had gossiped. From mouth to mouth the story had
spread . . . through the Guards, from club to club, from one
royal court of Europe to the next. Now it had come to
Stockmar's ever-open ears and he saw it as his duty to inform
Bertie's parents.

Stockmar had heard also about the meeting at Speyer. He
understood, he wrote to Albert, that it was hoped "that the
defects of spirit and mind of one person should be made up by
the strength of the other". Carefully naming no names, he
queried whether "the other" possessed the necessary qualities;
doubted whether the proposed marriage would work.

"What we know for certain is only youth and beauty," he
wrote. "I am wondering whether the important moral powers
we need are available as well."

But Albert, at this moment, was less concerned with Alix's
possible strength of character than with this fresh evidence of
Bertie's lack of it.

His face drawn, bald and prematurely aged at forty-two,
stooping a little as though he found his self-imposed duties as
Prince Consort too heavy for him, he hurried along to his wife's
sitting room with Stockmar's letter.

Queen Victoria, like her husband, was shocked and horrified.
There was, of course, a slight possibility that Stockmar was
misinformed.

Albert promptly proceeded to make his own inquiries. He did

not have to go far. Even if he and the Queen had not heard the story of Nellie Clifden until now, nearly everyone else at court had. A tell-tale courtier was only too eager to repeat it.

Again the Prince Consort hurried to his wife's room. Withholding only what he considered the more "disgusting details" of Bertie's escapade, he told her what he had learned.

They decided he must write immediately to Bertie at Cambridge. Was this, the letter demanded to know, the real reason for his strange reluctance to marry?

Bertie's reply was suitably penitent. He had yielded to temptation, he told his parents; he was deeply sorry and the affair was now definitely at an end. But he still hedged on the question of marriage.

Albert, at this time, was not well, suffering from what seemed to be a slight fever, tossing and turning restlessly at night, unable to sleep. Worrier that he was by nature, illness now caused him to visualize all sorts of ghosts and skeletons resulting from that night in Ireland when Nellie Clifden had crept, giggling, into Bertie's bed.

Suppose the wretched girl was with child? Suppose she brought a paternity suit against Bertie? Albert's fears quickly communicated themselves to Queen Victoria. They decided to go to Cambridge so that Albert could talk to his son face to face, man to man. They travelled by special train and stayed overnight with Bertie at Madingley Hall. But what passed between father and son upset Albert rather more than it did Bertie. He returned to Windsor quite exhausted and "at a very low ebb", as he put it himself.

He was still feverish; unable to sleep. His head ached intolerably and there were pains in his body which he put down to rheumatism. It was, in fact, something much more serious. The Prince Consort was ill with typhoid, almost certainly contracted from the bad drains and putrid cesspools as common to Windsor Castle as to the slums of the big cities.

A week after returning from Cambridge it became increasingly clear that Albert was a desperately sick man. Two physicians, James Clark and William Jenner, were called in. If they knew that the Prince Consort had typhoid, they kept it to themselves.

Queen Victoria was beside herself with worry. As Albert became increasingly delirious, as the doctors tried in vain to check the fever, she hovered around his bedside, white-faced and sobbing. Only with difficulty could she be persuaded to leave him at all; to go to her own room and try to snatch a few hours' sleep.

More doctors were called in. To no avail. It became increasingly clear that the Prince Consort was dying. It was suggested to Queen Victoria that she should send for Bertie.

Obstinately, she shook her head. Not understanding, perhaps not realizing even now that it was typhoid from which her beloved Albert was suffering, she blamed her eldest son for his father's illness. It was all Bertie's fault—his idleness and his loose ways, that wretched business in Ireland. To see Bertie, she was sure, would only make poor Albert worse.

It was his eighteen-year-old sister Alice who finally, secretly, without Queen Victoria knowing, sent Bertie the telegram which summoned him home to Windsor.

The telegram reached him late at night. He travelled through the night from Cambridge and arrived at Windsor Castle at three o'clock in the morning.

It seemed at first as though Bertie's arrival had coincided with a change for the better. At six o'clock on the morning of 14th December, a Saturday, Queen Victoria was awakened with the glad tidings that Albert's fever had broken and the crisis was over.

An hour later it became tragically all too clear that this was not the case, and at eleven o'clock that night, with his wife clutching his hand, Alice on his other side, Bertie and Lenchen huddled together at the foot of the bed, Prince Albert died.

Queen Victoria was frantic with grief, sobbing hysterically, in a state of near collapse. Half walking, half carried, she was taken through to the Red Room and helped on to a sofa. Her sobs were heart-rending.

She was still sobbing, white faced, her eyes dark rimmed with tragedy and tiredness, when Bertie went in to see her.

"I will be all I can to you, Mama," he pledged himself.

Queen Victoria was never to forget her beloved Albert; and it was to be a long time before she was to cease to blame Bertie for his father's death. But the funeral over, she was more than ever determined that her eldest son should marry Princess Alix—after a suitable period of mourning, of course. Albert had given the proposed match his blessing. To her, from the very first day of their marriage, Albert's word had been law and never more so than now that he was dead.

"I feel it is sacred duty he, our darling angel, left us to perform," she wrote to Vicky.

Vicky agreed with her that now, more than ever, what Bertie needed most was a wife who would keep him straight. "As he is too weak to keep from sin for virtue's sake, he will only keep out of it from other motives and surely a wife will be the strongest," she wrote back.

Blaming Bertie for his father's death, the Queen could not bear to have her eldest son around her. She sent him off to tour Egypt and Palestine accompanied by a list of do's and don'ts such as Albert might have drafted had he been still alive. Bertie was to travel incognito, listen to a sermon each Sunday he was away and read only good books.

Penitent in the immediate aftermath of his father's death, Bertie was more than willing to do whatever Mama wished even in the matter of marriage.

"I only trust that everything will succeed according to your wishes and that you will be pleased with the young Princess when you see her," he wrote home in the course of his travels.

To his mother's delight, he was still seemingly of the same mind when he returned at the end of his five-months' trip. He had grown a beard while he was away. It made him look both older and more handsome. The trip had benefited him in other ways, too. He was "much less coarse looking and the expression of his eyes so much better", his mother noted.

He had also taken to smoking a pipe, but this his mother, who abhorred smoking, did not know.

The idea of marrying and having children no longer frightened him, as it had done in the weeks immediately following the Nellie Clifden episode. He was ready and willing to marry Alix at any time. Indeed, in Paris, on his way back, he had gone shopping and bought her a number of small gifts as an expression of his feelings.

He was, all at once, "amiable, good and sensible", Queen Victoria concluded.

BETROTHAL

Outwardly composed, inwardly nervous, Alix sat with her parents in King Leopold's writing room at Laeken Palace in Belgium. In the next room, a small boudoir, waiting to meet her, was the bereaved and awe-inspiring Queen Victoria.

It was 3rd September 1862 and Alix, as on the occasion of her visit to Speyer nearly a year before, was wearing a new dress. A much prettier dress than she normally wore. Usually, for reasons of economy, her dresses were plain and simple. But young Mrs Paget, who had done much towards arranging this meeting at Laeken just as she had for the earlier ones with Vicky at Strelitz and Bertie at Speyer, had suggested she should wear something pretty. She had also impressed upon the girl that she should be as quiet as possible, which was not difficult for Alix, and that on no account must she permit herself to laugh.

The bereaved Queen Victoria could "hardly bear to see a laughing face", Wally Paget cautioned her.

Alix had known nothing of the true purpose of that supposed sightseeing visit to Speyer cathedral a year before. But she knew now, quite clearly, what this visit to Laeken portended. She was to marry the Prince of Wales. Well, perhaps. Much depended upon what his mother, Queen Victoria, thought of her when they met in a few more minutes.

For months past, whenever the opportunity had presented itself, Princess Louise had allowed the name of the Prince of Wales to creep into conversation with her daughter, sounding her out, gauging her reactions, trying to read into Alix's teenage blushes the true extent of her feelings. They were, inevitably, confused feelings, as Bertie's were, but for very different reasons. Alix was, of course, flattered and excited, as what young girl would not have been. Bertie, after all, was the Prince of Wales and England's future King. But the honour being done to her if the marriage went forward and the new status she would enjoy in the future did not weigh heavily with her. She was not that sort of girl. Love—that he should love her and she him—was more important.

"I'd hate it to be an arranged marriage," she told her mother. "That would be a terrible thing."

But if he really did love her, if he wanted to marry her, her mother said—what then?

"If he really loves me—yes."

A letter from Vicky brought her reassurance. If Bertie's feelings were not all they should be, "it would not have gone as far as this", Bertie's sister wrote, confidently.

Alix, of course, knew nothing of Bertie's amorous escapade in Ireland, though her parents did. The whole of royal Europe buzzed with the story and Queen Victoria was worried that Alix's parents might yet call things off if they got the wrong impression of the "scrape" (as she now thought of it) into which her "poor innocent boy" had been led by "wicked wretches". She wrote to Wally, asking her to see Alix's parents and put the whole unhappy business into the right perspective.

Wally did so and arrangements again went smoothly, if slowly, forward. It was arranged that Alix and her parents should spend a short holiday at Ostend. While there, King Leopold would invite them to Laeken Palace where Queen Victoria, having just married off her second daughter, Alice, to Prince Louis of Hesse, would be staying overnight on her way to visit her dead husband's birthplace.

Everything had gone as planned. The next move lay with Queen Victoria. Wally Paget went through to the next room to fetch her.

The Queen, as always, was dressed in deepest mourning, looking older than her years and far more formidable than she really was. She was, indeed, as she was to confess later, as shy and nervous of meeting Alix as Alix was of meeting her. She hoped she was going to like the girl and felt sure she was. Yet another letter from Vicky had reassured her about Alix: "No brilliancy of wit or talent . . . very shy . . . the peacemaker of the family; someone who did her duty, whether pleasant or not, unswervingly."

Wally told the Queen that the others were ready for her. But Queen Victoria was lost in thought, her mind going back, as it did often, to dear, dead Albert.

"You, dear Wally," she said, "will quite understand what I feel at this moment. You have a husband you love and know what I have lost."

With that, she burst into tears.

It took her a few moments to regain her composure. She dried
her eyes and stood up, telling Mrs Paget to lead on into the next
room and announce her.

Wally did as she was bid and the Queen followed her into the
drawing room where Alix and her parents were waiting. It was
almost exactly half-past one.

It was, as it was bound to be, a somewhat awkward and
perhaps slightly embarrassing encounter on both sides, which
Princess Louise's deafness did nothing to help. Wally Paget,
having announced the Queen, discreetly withdrew and it was left
to King Leopold's daughter-in-law, the Duchess of Brabant, to
do her best to thaw the regal ice. She did not entirely succeed
and even Queen Victoria admitted later that she found the going
"stiff".

Stiff though the going may have been, the Queen was immediately charmed by Alix, as indeed was nearly everyone who
ever met her. "Lovely . . . quiet . . . ladylike"—these were the
adjectives with which Queen Victoria, later, in private, summed
her up.

The ice of embarrassment might perhaps have thawed further
if the Queen had joined the others for the luncheon which King
Leopold had thoughtfully arranged. But she did not. Preferring
to be alone with her memories and her grief, she lunched apart
with her small daughter, Beatrice. But she confided in Wally
Paget that she was favourably impressed and Wally passed this
information on to Alix's mother—as perhaps Queen Victoria
intended her to do.

But if the Queen was already charmed by her future daughter-
in-law, she was to be completely captivated by her that evening.
She was upstairs in her room when Alix came in to see her. The
girl was wearing a simple black dress unadorned by any sort of
embroidery or jewellery, her soft brown hair hanging down
about her shoulders in long ringlets. Her whole appearance was
one of the utmost simplicity, dignity and charm. Nothing could
have appealed more strongly to the bereaved and sorrowing
Queen, and her eyes, as she looked at Alix and thought back on
her own first meeting with Albert, were misted afresh with tears.

A more emotional woman than her somewhat forbidding
outward appearance may have suggested, her whole heart went
out to Alix at that moment. She beckoned the girl to her and

handed her a small sprig of white heather. Bertie himself had picked it at Balmoral, she said.

"I hope it will bring you luck," said the Queen.

The next day, before resuming her journey to Coburg, she saw Alix's parents. To them she expressed the hope that Alix, if she saw fit to accept Bertie, would do so "with her whole heart and will".

Not to be outdone, Princess Louise replied that Bertie might indeed hope that Alix would do so and added the hope that Bertie too felt "a real inclination".

It was thus left, theoretically at least, for Bertie to propose only if he felt so inclined and for Alix to accept or reject him as her heart dictated. But neither parent had the slightest doubt that Bertie would propose and Alix would accept.

Alix's parents expressed their conviction that Alix would make Bertie a good wife, and be a comfort to his widowed mother.

Yes, she would be entering a very sad household, the Queen told them.

With the Queen's departure for Coburg, Alix and her parents left Laeken Palace to return to their hotel in Ostend. They did not have long to wait. Bertie arrived the following day, fresh from visiting his newly-acquired estate at Sandringham. He was accompanied by his newly-appointed Comptroller, General Knollys. The two of them stopped overnight at the same hotel in which Alix and her parents were staying.

It was Bertie's first meeting with Alix's parents and he made a good impression upon them. "One of the most charming young men I have met," Prince Christian said of him. Bertie went on to Brussels. Two days later Alix and her parents joined him there and all four had lunch together. In Bertie's presence, Alix was as bright and gay as her parents had ever seen her. "She is much in love with him," her father remarked.

Lunch over, Bertie suggested that Prince Christian should join him in his hotel room. Bertie came quickly to the point. He loved Alix, he told her father, and wished to marry her.

"Are you quite sure?" Prince Christian asked him.

"I have quite made up my mind," Bertie assured him.

Later that day, after they had all been for a short drive together, Bertie saw Alix's mother. He told her, as he had told Alix's father, that he loved their daughter and wished to marry her.

"I know you will be kind to her," said Princess Louise.

"He seems truly in love with her," Alix's father confided later.

So the stage was set. Queen Victoria had given her approval; Alix's parents had given their consent. It remained only for Bertie to propose. He did so the following day, 9th September.

So romantic an occasion required an equally romantic setting. Uncle Leopold supplied it by inviting them again to Laeken. After lunch Bertie asked Alix to take a walk with him in the palace gardens. They came to the grotto. There, as though by mutual consent, they stopped.

But Bertie, now that the moment had actually come, found himself tongue-tied. Alix eased the situation by mentioning the sprig of white heather his mother had given her.

He said what his mother had said: "I hope it will bring you good luck."

He asked her if she liked England.

Alix did not know. She had never been there, she told him.

Would you like to go?

"Oh, yes," she said, eagerly.

"When you do come to England," Bertie said, "I hope you will remain there always." He paused. Then came the question: "Will you marry me?"

"Yes," Alix replied, unhesitatingly.

Custom and courtesy required that he should offer her time for consideration. There was no need for so quick an answer, he said. She could have time to think it over if she wished.

"I have thought things over," Alix told him with child-like frankness. "Long ago."

"You like me, then?"

"Oh, yes."

He took her hand and kissed it. She kissed him in return.

They walked on together, talking of Bertie's mother—"She will love you as her own daughter"—and of his dead father.

"I hope he would have approved of your choice," said Alix.

"It was always his greatest wish," Bertie assured her. "My only fear is that I am not worthy of you."

They returned to the palace where Bertie again asked Alix's parents—formally this time—for their daughter's hand. Then he kissed her again and she kissed him in return. She tucked her

hand affectionately through his arm for a photograph to commemorate the occasion.

"I still feel as if I was in a dream . . ." Bertie wrote to his
mother. "I really don't know if I am on my head or my heels . . .
If only I can prove to dear Alix that I am not unworthy of her
love and make her future a happy one, I think I shall have every
reason to be content."

That evening Uncle Leopold gave a small banquet to celebrate
their betrothal. In the days that followed Bertie and Alix went
riding together and on a sort of betrothal outing to view the
battlefield of Waterloo which Bertie very much wanted to see.
Of an evening, Alix played the piano for him and sang in her
husky voice. After the fashion of the day, they were permitted to
be alone together only if the door of the room was left open.
Queen Victoria had also left orders that Bertie was on no account
to return to Copenhagen with Alix. Their marriage was to be
personal, not political, and for him to visit Denmark might be
construed in Germany as indicating otherwise. There would be
quite enough huffing and puffing in Germany as it was. In this,
Queen Victoria was undeniably right. Vicky and Fritz apart,
those in Germany were not at all pleased at the news of the
betrothal. But in England the announcement was greeted with
delight and enthusiasm.

Obedient to his mother's word, Bertie travelled with Alix and
her parents only as far as Cologne. There he said goodbye and
went off to join Mama in Coburg. Loving letters from Alix, each
several pages long, pursued him.

"The match is really quite a love match," Uncle Leopold
wrote delightedly to his niece, Victoria. "Bertie is extremely
happy and in admiration of his very lovely young bride. All the
arguments that one forced him to marry a young lady he had
never even seen fall most completely to the ground."

"I only now know what it is to be really happy," Bertie
himself confided to a cousin in Coburg.

A VISIT TO OSBORNE

If Alix was nervous and ill-at-ease as she came ashore from the ship *Black Eagle* on the evening of 5th November 1862, it could hardly be wondered at. The prospect ahead of her was enough to daunt the heart of any young girl. She was to spend the next few weeks alone with her future mother-in-law at Osborne, the royal house of mourning on the Isle of Wight.

The fact that her father was with her was of but little comfort. He was to stay only two nights. So Queen Victoria had ordained. As for her mother . . . she was not to come at all. Nor was the girl to bring a lady-in-waiting or personal maid of her own nationality with her. And Bertie, Alix knew, would not be at Osborne. He had been packed off on a Mediterranean cruise aboard one of the royal yachts. His mother wanted no other influences at work during this crucial period when she proposed to mould her future daughter-in-law in the correct image of a Princess of Wales.

Bertie, to his credit, had protested to his mother when he learned what was planned. Unable to budge her, he even appealed to King Leopold to intervene. Leopold did. It would be a considerable ordeal for someone as young as Alix, he wrote to his royal niece, and it was no way to treat a future King and Queen of Denmark to say that one should stay only two nights and the other could not come at all.

But Queen Victoria was not to be swayed. She wanted her future daughter-in-law to herself and that was the way it was going to be.

As Alix and her father came ashore, two of the Queen's children were waiting on the quayside to greet them, the teenage Helena (known as Lenchen) and little Leopold, the nine-year-old haemophilic, so delicate of skin as to be almost transparent looking.

Tall for his age, affectionate by nature, Leo had brought a bouquet of flowers with him to welcome Alix. Overcome by emotion, she took the boy impulsively in her arms and kissed him.

They all climbed into the waiting carriage and set off for Osborne, where the Queen awaited them with two more of her children, Louise, aged fourteen, and Baby, the youngest. If Alix was nervous, so too perhaps was the Queen. Either nerves or excitement made her unable to eat, except for a few spoonfuls of soup, once she heard that Alix's ship had been sighted.

It had been delayed by fog. But now the fog had lifted and moonlight bathed the oaks, elms and beeches as Alix and her father drove towards Osborne, that strangely Italian-looking villa overlooking the Solent which the dead Albert had designed as an away-from-it-all home for himself and Victoria.

Alix was looking well and lovely, the Queen told her as she led her upstairs to the room which had been prepared for her. Later that evening, with the younger children tucked away in bed, they dined together, the Queen and Lenchen, Alix and her father, beneath Landseer's painting of *The Deer Drive* in the Council Room.

It rained all next day and the children took the opportunity to show Alix round the house, tugging her by the hand through the marble-tiled corridors to a succession of long, lofty rooms crowded with furniture and congested with portraits, miniatures, vases, busts and porcelain. The entwined initials V and A were everywhere.

Next day the rain cleared and Queen Victoria took her for a drive through the grounds, pausing to admire the fountains and statues, the winding walks, the Christmas trees and monkey puzzle trees which the dead Albert had imported from his native Germany.

After two nights, in accordance with Queen Victoria's imperious decision, Alix's father said goodbye to her and left for home. Outside, a raging gale beat in from the sea and it was again pouring with rain. Alix, watching her father go with a sad heart, was finally alone in that gloomy house, hushed in mourning and stiff with etiquette. The children afforded her some small degree of youthful company and with Lenchen in particular, because she was nearest to her own age, she was quickly good friends. But voices must always be kept low and youthful laughter quickly hushed out of respect for Mama's grief. Alix, with that "sweet" disposition which Vicky had noted and mentioned in one of her letters, understood and sympathized.

Yet Alix's nature was more than merely sympathetic and understanding. It was also, at one and the same time, compliant and resilient. Thanks to all these qualities, the visit passed off surprisingly well. If Alix felt at all homesick for her native Denmark, she kept her feelings well hidden . . . as later she was to keep other, deeper feelings hidden from Bertie.

She showed herself eager to please, willing to learn, anxious to fit herself in every possible way for her future position as Princess of Wales. Daily she practised her English, her reading and writing, her drawing. Every night she went to bed sharp at ten o'clock.

The Queen ordained and Alix complied. The Queen talked and Alix listened. More and more, as the visit progressed, she endeared herself to her future mother-in-law. The Queen found her "gentle, good, simple, unspoilt, thoroughly honest and straight-forward—so affectionate". And one night, in the Queen's bedroom with its chintz coverings and heavy mahogany furniture, Alix could no longer hold back her tears as the Queen talked, as she so often did, about her dead, dear Albert and the happy days now gone forever. At this moment, perhaps more than any other, Alix won a lasting place in the Queen's heart. "This jewel", Queen Victoria called her.

From Osborne the Queen and her Court moved to Windsor Castle, where the Prince Consort had died and where his sorrowing widow still did all in her power to keep his spirit alive. In his bedroom the glass from which he had taken his last sip of medicine still stood by the bedside. Each evening fresh clothes were laid out for him on his bed and a fresh jug of hot water was carried into his dressing room as though he still lived and would shortly be down for dinner.

It was hardly the gayest of atmospheres for a bride-to-be not yet eighteen. But it was brighter than Osborne and briefly brightened still further by a visit from the Cambridge family. With their arrival, talk turned from the subject of the dead Albert to the question of the forthcoming wedding . . . how many bridesmaids there should be (eight), what Alix would need by way of a trousseau and where the honeymoon should be spent. Osborne, of course. Queen Victoria quickly decided that, as she was to decide almost everything else about her son's marriage.

Having come to know and love her future daughter-in-law, Queen Victoria was loth to part with her. Bertie was due back from his Mediterranean cruise early in December and the Queen suggested that Alix should stay on and see him. Alix, like any other young girl in love, was eager to do so. But her parents, when they heard of the Queen's suggestion, did not agree at all. Perhaps they felt that Queen Victoria, for the time being, had had things sufficiently her own way. Alix must return home in time for her birthday celebrations on 1st December they wrote. Queen Victoria, to whom birthdays were a near-sacred institution, could not but agree.

Again Alix's father journeyed from Denmark. Again he was treated with scant courtesy by the Queen. There was no room for him at Windsor Castle, she said, and he was forced to stay at the Danish embassy instead.

Hearing that Alix would be leaving before he was back, Bertie wrote that he would meet her in Lille and travel with her—a suggestion which brought a quick reminder from Mama that he must on no account go to Denmark.

Bertie did as his mother commanded. He met Alix and her father at Lille, travelled with them to Cologne and Hanover, then said goodbye. He and Alix were not to see each other again until a few days before the wedding. Over a space of eighteen months they had met on only three occasions and seen each other for a total of little more than two weeks in all.

The wedding day was fixed for 10th March. The Queen, still mourning Albert and not yet ready to face the people of London, decided that the ceremony would take place in St George's chapel at Windsor. Nine hundred guests would be invited, but only eight from the bride's side, Alix's parents, her brothers and sisters, and two uncles.

The Queen was equally autocratic over the question of who Alix should bring with her into her new life as Princess of Wales. No one at all. There must be no Danish lady-in-waiting to encourage her to talk in her own language (which Bertie did not understand); no little Danish maid even. Ladies-in-waiting and maids alike must be of sound English stock. The Queen picked them herself, among them Lady Macclesfield whose total of children ran into double figures and who might therefore be expected to give Alix a few pointers on the delicate subjects of marriage and motherhood.

Marlborough House in Pall Mall, the Queen decided, would

make a suitable town house for the Prince and Princess of Wales. For a country house, there was Sandringham, a white-fronted Georgian mansion with a run-down estate of some 7000 acres on the windswept Norfolk coast. It had been bought some nine months earlier at a cost of £220,000, with a further £60,000 set aside for necessary royal improvements.

Purchase and improvements had made a considerable dent in the £600,000 of acrued revenues from the Duchy of Cornwall which were part and parcel of Bertie's birthright. The Duchy revenues, at this time, were running at something like £62,000 a year, no mean sum in an era when a middle-class family could live in comfort, with three or four servants and their own carriage, on £1000 a year. But for Bertie, the Queen felt, it was not enough.

At her instigation, Parliament granted him a further £40,000 a year on marriage with an additional £10,000 a year for Alix. It was a considerable sum, *The Times* pointed out, and Bertie would be expected to live up to it; to entertain lavishly. Bertie, as time was quickly to show, was only too happy to oblige.

"THEY DON'T KNOW ME YET"

An ice-cold wind swept through the streets of Copenhagen that February day in 1863 when Alix, in accordance with Queen Victoria's edict that she must be in Brussels by 2nd March and in London by the 7th, said goodbye to her native Denmark. Understandable tears glistened in her blue eyes. Yet she was not completely sad and downcast at this moment of parting from familiar things. Excitement, too, bubbled inside her.

Copenhagen, its streets gay with bunting, matched her mood as she and her parents drove to the railway station. She was wearing a dress of brown and white striped silk and one of those "natty little bonnets which seem to sit better on her head than anybody else's", as Wally Paget noted. She had made the bonnet herself.

In Brussels, King Leopold sent ten state carriages to meet her. The same ten carriages took her again to the railway station three days later, with Belgium's Grand Marshal deputed to accompany

Alix and Bertie on their wedding day, 10th March 1863

Sandringham before its rebuilding 1868–70

Bertie and Alix at Sandringham, 1864

her to Antwerp, where the royal yacht *Victoria and Albert* was waiting.

Punctually on 7th March, a cold, grey, wintry day, to the accompaniment of a salute of guns and the roared approval or the crowds thronging the banks, the royal yacht steamed up the Thames and dropped anchor at Gravesend. From her cabin Alix looked out on the strange new country which was to be her future home.

For once in his life, Bertie, normally a very punctual young man, was late. Agitated and nervous, he had left Windsor at half-past nine that morning. But he was delayed on the way and it was twenty minutes after the appointed time when he reached Gravesend. He found Alix, far from being upset by his lateness, thoroughly enjoying herself, darting from side to side of the royal yacht, waving happily in turn to the crowds on shore and the occupants of the armada of small craft which had sailed out to escort her up the Thames.

Out of deference to the widowed Victoria, she was wearing a half-mourning outfit, a crinoline dress of mauve-coloured silk and a matching jacket trimmed with sable. Her white bonnet was trimmed with rosebuds.

Bertie, in pale grey trousers and a navy blue overcoat, almost sprinted up the companionway. To everyone's delight, they kissed in full view of the watching crowds.

The streets of London were as gay with welcoming bunting as those of Copenhagen had been in farewell. If there were those who noticed that the carriages in the cavalcade were old and shabby, and who thought it a pretty poor turn-out, Alix did not. Excited and happy with Bertie beside her, she smiled brightly, bowing to right and left as they trotted along. So dense and enthusiastic were the crowds at one point that the escorting Life Guards had to use the flats of their sabres to clear a path. So great was the crush that the Lord Mayor of London, pushing through to welcome Alix, lost the rest of his party in the crowd.

A Life Guard and his horse, slipping on the shiny cobbles, went down with a crash. A woman, fearful of being crushed by the crowd, deftly passed her baby to the surprised occupants of one of the carriages. A small boy somehow got his arm caught in the spokes of Alix's carriage as it came to a halt. She leaned quickly over and disentangled him before the procession moved on again.

Modest and unassuming as she was, she could hardly credit that she was the cause of all this excitement.

"It must be for the Prince of Wales," she said. "They don't know me yet."

So dense were the crowds that it was five o'clock before they reached Paddington station. At Slough Bertie's brothers were waiting to greet them. It was seven o'clock, dark, with the rain pouring down, before they reached Windsor Castle.

They entered the castle amidst a flurry of welcomes and greetings. It seemed as if everyone was trying to talk at once. Alix, for the first time, began to feel tired. Then, suddenly, everyone was silent.

Alix looked up and there was Queen Victoria, not quite at the bottom of the stairs, her small, black-garbed figure seeming to tower over them all. Bertie took Alix by the hand and led her to where his mother was standing.

The Queen embraced her warmly, then turned and led her and the rest of the party upstairs to the White Drawing Room. As so often in moments of family importance, the Queen, missing Albert, was battling with her emotions. Soon, she went to her own room. There, alone, torn by emotion, she gave way finally to tears and it was left to Vicky, who had journeyed from Berlin for her brother's wedding, to show Alix and her parents to the rooms which had been prepared for them.

Sympathetic and understanding as always, Alix knew how the Queen was feeling. Later, when she had rested, she went along to the Queen's room and tapped gently on the door. The Queen and Vicky were alone together, dressing for dinner. Alix went into the room and crossed to where the Queen was sitting. Without saying a word, she knelt dutifully in front of her.

The Queen was deeply moved. She sank down beside Alix, crushed her to her and kissed her again and again in a welter of emotion.

PART TWO

Wedded Bliss

"I WOULD LOVE HIM JUST THE SAME"

The wedding day—10th March 1863—sparkled with frost and sunlight. In different parts of Windsor Castle, Alix and Bertie were alike up early. Bertie's boyish face, with its protuberant eyes and drooping lids, was pale with nerves as he put on his general's uniform and the heavy, rich Garter robe in which he was to be married. Alix, for her part, was torn by conflicting, eighteen-year-old emotions as she donned her wedding dress of silver tissue trimmed with Honiton lace.

Like any other young bride, she was, by turns, eager and excited, nervous and tense. Love for Bertie battled with home-sickness for her native Denmark. At one stage of the long, four-hour process of getting dressed for her wedding she burst briefly into tears at the thought that she was parting from her parents and her future life was to be lived out in a strange land. Then love for Bertie reasserted itself and she brushed away her tears. She was marrying him for love, not for the status it would bring her as Princess of Wales, she volunteered to Vicky when the bridegroom's sister popped her head round the door to see how things were coming along. "If he were a cowboy, I would love him just the same," said Alix, emotionally.

But the tensest, most nervous person in Windsor Castle that morning was Queen Victoria. The fact that this was her eldest son's wedding day was permitted to make no difference to the way she dressed. Her love for the dead Albert still over-rode everything else and she dressed, as always, in deepest mourning. Unable to face the public, she declined to take any part in the pre-marital processions. Instead, hemmed in by her ladies-in-waiting, she walked to St George's chapel by a special covered way, slipping quietly and unobtrusively into the Royal Closet with its drapes of purple and gold. From there, as from a box in a theatre, she could look down on the marriage ceremony . . . and the dead Albert could look down with her. He was with her in spirit if not in fact. The badge of the Order of the Garter which she wore on her mourning dress had been his. The Victoria and Albert Order, which she also wore, had been re-fashioned so that his head now surmounted hers. And the diamond brooch she wore contained a portrait of him in miniature.

Tension made the Queen restless as she looked down on the colourful pagentry below ... the backcloth of knightly banners, the scarlet-clad Beefeaters in their medieval attire, the heralds in scarlet and gold, the state trumpeters in cloth-of-gold, the guests—the men mostly in uniform, the ladies gowned and bejewelled in wedding-day finery. Her small, black-gloved hands toyed endlessly with her veil. From time to time she stirred restlessly in her chair. She could not sit still and quivered visibly as a shrill blast of trumpets heralded the arrival of her daughters in the semi-mourning she had ordained that they should wear. Only once did she smile—the small, proud smile of motherhood—as she glimpsed her youngest child, the golden-haired Baby, bringing up at the rear of the procession of princesses.

A second shrill blast from the state trumpeters announced the arrival of the bridegroom, flanked by his 'supporters'—his brother-in-law, Fritz, the Crown Prince of Prussia, and his uncle, the Duke of Saxe-Coburg, who, while opposed to the marriage, had no wish to be left out of the actual wedding ceremony. Bertie bowed in the direction of the Queen, half-hidden in the shadows of the Royal Closet. His face drained of colour, he continued to cast anxious glances in her direction as he, and everyone else, awaited the arrival of the bride. Overcome by the emotion of the moment, his sister, Vicky, burst unashamedly into tears. She had her small son, the four-year-old Willy, with his withered arm, a heritage of childbirth, by the hand. Now she let go and, boy-like, he was soon busy nipping the legs of his youthful kilted uncles, Arthur and Leopold, much to Queen Victoria's concern. Too hard a nip might perhaps set off the 'bleeding disease' from which little Leopold suffered.

Finally, the bride and her attendant bridesmaids. Slowly and gracefully in her dress of silver tissue, a diamond diadem on her head, Alix seemed to float rather than walk up the aisle to where

Bertie awaited her, her face "very pale but full of awe and wonder", as Charles Dickens reported.

As the organ burst into the Chorale, which Bertie's dead father had written, it was Queen Victoria's turn to dissolve in tears. She rose from her seat and vanished briefly into the shadows at the rear of the Royal Closet to compose herself. The Archbishop of Canterbury, four bishops and the Dean of Windsor all played a part in the marriage service. For all that, Queen Victoria thought it "a sad, dismal ceremony". But that was perhaps a reflection of her own sad thoughts. Alix, as the service ran its course, was visibly trembling at Bertie's side, but her responses, though quiet, were clear-cut and sure to those close enough to hear them.

When it was all over, they stood there a moment, the young bride and groom, looking up at Bertie's mother in her perch in the Royal Closet. The Queen gave Bertie a small, motherly nod. Then, lifting her black-gloved hand, she kissed it in Alix's direction.

Bertie and Alix arrived back at Windsor Castle to find the Queen waiting to greet them. More composed, less emotional than she had been during the service, she embraced them warmly in turn. Then, turning, she led the way upstairs to the White Drawing Room where they signed the marriage register. But just as she had taken no part in the procession or ceremony, so she declined to join them for the wedding luncheon with its huge wedding cake, taller than either Alix or Bertie. Instead, she lunched apart with only her small daughter, Baby, for company. However, she did join them again after lunch in the Green Drawing Room.

Alix, by now, had changed into her going-away outfit—a dress of white silk with a lace shawl and a white bonnet trimmed with orange flowers; an ermine mantle and muff against the outside cold. Though the wedding itself was over, she seemed now, somehow, more highstrung and agitated than ever as she said goodbye to her parents, to her brothers and and sisters. Gone forever was the old, sometimes impoverished but always warmly close-knit family life in Copenhagen. Ahead lay a new, totally different life as the wife of the Prince of Wales. With Bertie, she climbed into the waiting carriage and they were off on the first stage of their journey to Osborne House for a not-quite-two-weeks' honeymoon.

They were not, however, to be left entirely alone. Vicky intruded briefly upon them before returning to Prussia with Fritz and Willy.

"Bertie looks blissful," she reported to their mother. "I never saw such a change." Alix, she added, looked charming and lovely, but then she always did.

"Love has certainly shed its sunshine on these two dear young hearts," wrote Vicky, waxing almost poetic . . . and this time she added nothing about not envying the girl who was now her brother's wife.

THE GAY LIFE

The ball given by the Brigade of Guards in honour of the newly-married Prince and Princess of Wales in the picture gallery of the International Exhibition at Kensington on 26th June was generally acknowledged to be the most splendidly glittering occasion of the London season. All the men looked handsome in their uniforms and none more so than Bertie. All the ladies looked beautiful and none more beautiful than Alix, a jewelled diadem glittering on her head, her gown of white lace over mauve looking little like the half-mourning it was supposed to be. Everyone who was anyone in Society was there that night and the jewels which glittered at the throats and wrists of the ladies present were said to be worth a king's ransom. Certainly the gold plate, which decorated the picture gallery was worth something like £2 million and even Queen Victoria had honoured the occasion, if not with her presence, with the loan of tapestries and other valuables from the Buckingham Palace she so seldom visited.

For Alix and Bertie it was a wonderfully exciting occasion— and never more wonderful and exciting than when the officers of the regiments formed two long lines, their swords flashing in a triumphal arch beneath which the young, newly-married guests of honour floated rather than danced the length of the gallery. Bertie was flushed with pride and pleasure; Alix radiant with happiness.

On that night—or on another very like it and very close to it in time—Alix conceived her first child.

Whatever may have happened before or after, they were, at this time, both very much in love, idolizing each other, gay and happy not only in their marriage but as the acknowledged and undoubted leaders of London's aristocratic social set. The London season that year of 1863, everyone agreed, was gayer, more hectic and more expensive than ever before. For those with money and the entry to fashionable society, there were, every day, drives in the park, luncheon parties, dinner parties, opera and ballet, a choice of four or five balls a night. And most splendid and popular of all were those functions graced by the gay young Prince and Princess of Wales.

Their new home at Marlborough House, into which they moved at the end of May, was quickly the focal point of fashionable life, though alterations and renovations were still not complete. New coach-houses and stables were being built to accommodate extra carriages and horses. A new porte-cochere and hall were added to provide a more imposing entrance. The former entrance hall was transformed into a handsome reception room with a white marble fireplace and tapestried walls. Three other rooms were knocked into one to form a vast pillared drawing room with twin fireplaces and walls hung with pale pink silk. Numerous mirrors made for lightness and brightness, with pale blue blinds at the windows to ward off the sun in summer. The removal of the plaster in the old reception hall and on the adjoining stairway brought to light long-forgotten paintings by Louis Laguerre of Marlborough's battles and sieges. Delightedly, Bertie had them restored.

Before moving in to Marlborough House, they journeyed to Norfolk to see how their new country home at Sandringham was coming along. They travelled by the Great Eastern Line from Shoreditch to King's Lynn where a carriage was waiting to convey them the last few miles. It was Alix's first visit to Sandringham and there was a stimulating smell of the sea in the air as they clip-clopped over the little stone bridge spanning the Babingley river and crossed the open heathland beyond.

Tall pines and massed rhododendrons served as a natural windbreak to the house. They broke free of the trees and Alix saw for the first time the three-storeyed Georgian mansion, white-fronted and slate-roofed in those days, with its dozens of chimneys and its ornate, out-jutting porch. At that moment she fell completely in love with Sandringham, house and countryside alike. Everything about the place—its haphazard mixture of heathland and farmland, woodland and heath, the stiff, bracing winds gusting in from the North Sea, the smell of the sea in the air—reminded her strongly of her native Denmark. Here, more than anywhere else, she was to feel at home during the often unhappy years which lay ahead.

But unhappiness had no place in her thoughts—and Bertie had not yet developed a wandering eye—during that first visit to Sandringham. They were delighted with everything about the place and even the temporary discomforts of the visit seemed a pleasure rather than a penance. Builders were still at work on alterations and extensions and they had to stay in a handful of rooms furnished with items the previous owner had left behind.

Back in London, they moved into Marlborough House and began furnishing to their own taste. They furnished it, as far as possible, with homemade products: silk from Spitalfields, carpets from Wilton, damask from Manchester, furniture handmade in the small, cramped workshops of London's East End.

Alix, who had for so long shared a single small bedroom with her sister Minnie, now had a whole suite of rooms on the first floor all to herself in a mansion of over one hundred rooms. She had her own reception room with walls of cream figured tussore silk. She had a boudoir with red damask curtains and chintz-covered walls which she quickly filled with family photographs. Here she had her piano. There were two more pianos—concert grands—in the vast drawing room downstairs. A bonbonnière held a selection of her favourite sweetmeats. Her dressing room, with furnishings of light Hungarian oak, was similarly chintzy. Bertie's dressing room, by contrast, when it was built on later, had walls decorated with white polka-dots on a blue ground so that it looked not unlike a vast pocket handkerchief. Alix set aside another room for her painting and here she put up her two easels. Her private sitting room, downstairs, had a Chinese silk carpet on the floor, tapestries given to her by her mother-in-law on the walls and exquisite dwarf bookcases in mahogany and gold.

Like every other room in the house, it was crowded with furniture and cluttered with bric-à-brac. Upstairs, her dressing table was covered with scent bottles, trinkets, photographs and miniatures, The mantelpiece was crammed with everything from crudely-fashioned china pigs to the delicately-jewelled creations of the Russian master jeweller, Fabergé. Photographs were massed in ranks on her desk and at Sandringham, later, there were to be so many photographs on the grand piano that no one ever bothered to raise the lid.

A menagerie of pets filled the furniture-cluttered rooms of Marlborough House ... cats and dogs, cages holding canaries and bullfinches, an aquarium of goldfish. And everywhere there were Alix's favourite flowers, roses and carnations, tulips and pungent-smelling lilies-of-the-valley.

Bertie and Alix, at this early stage of married life, were like nothing so much as two small children playing 'house'. They were almost inseparable, breakfasting together in Alix's boudoir, having tea together on fine afternoons in basket chairs under the elms in the nearly five-acre garden.

Bertie's nineteen-year-old brother, Affie, was an early visitor to their new home. Indeed, his mother thought he was there far too much. She feared he was "smitten" with his attractive young sister-in-law and tried to discourage him. "It is like playing with fire," she wrote to Vicky.

Knowing Affie, as she knew Bertie, she feared that he might not have sufficient strength of either character or principle to resist temptation, and his subsequent dissipations were to prove her right. But if Affie lacked character and principle, Alix had enough of each for both of them. She was flattered by Affie's undisguised admiration, but there, for her, the matter ended.

For Alix, this was the brief peak period of married happiness. She was young and head over heels in love with Bertie. The whole world—at least, the world of fashionable London—was at her feet. At dances and parties, she was the belle of the ball, not only because she was Princess of Wales, but because she was elegantly beautiful in her own right. No longer was life so impecunious that she was compelled to make her own clothes. With her own £10,000 a year allowance—five times as much as her father received in Denmark—she could afford the best and latest of fashion. She had now a collection of jewellery any young woman might envy. Best of all, she had Bertie.

And he had her. Earlier he may have hedged over the question of marrying her. Later he was to be unfaithful. But now, during

these early months of marriage, he was completely captivated, as
everyone was, by her cool beauty, her huskily inviting voice and
deliciously broken accent. He idolized her.

"We have invited all the prettiest women we know." he told a
guest at one of the balls held at Marlborough House, "but the
Princess is the most beautiful of all."

Alix *was* beautiful. On that everyone was agreed. Bertie
basked happily in the reflected glory of her beauty, delighted at
the way everyone lionized her. If her conversation did not
exactly sparkle, if her wit was hardly diamond-bright, he did
not, as yet, notice. Or if he did, it did not seem to matter. There
were other things to do besides talk when they were alone
together. She satisfied both his husbandly pride and his masculine
needs . . . at least for the time being.

If marriage and the adulation to which they were subject
combined to turn both their heads, it was surely understandable.
Bertie, for the first time in his life, felt free of his mother's regal
apron-strings. Alix, for the first time in her life, was enjoying the
freedom and pleasures that money can bring. At Marlborough
House they entertained lavishly, formally in the state dining
room, a portrait of Queen Victoria over the white marble
mantelpiece at one end, a companion portrait of the dead
Prince Consort over the matching fireplace at the other end; less
formally in their private dining room with its walnut furnishings
and walls of green and gold. For state dinners, there was a
liveried page to wait on each royal guest and a page between
each pair of non-royal guests. Bertie himself was waited upon by
his valet, a massive six-footer whom he decked out in German
hunting costume, an idea copied from his dead father. But
whether the dinner party was formal or informal, it was always
Bertie, rather than Alix, who consulted with the chef concerning
the menu.

In the house itself and the vast, echoing basement beneath,
with its furnace room and china store, its linen room and
housekeeper's store, its silver pantry and wine cellar, Alix and
Bertie had eighty-five servants at their beck and call. Three or
four men did nothing else but clean and polish the silver plate.
Two more attended to the more than three hundred vases of
flowers. In the kitchen, a chef, two cooks and a confectioner
dealt with such delicacies as quail and ortolans, trout and sweet-

meats, while eight or nine kitchenmaids basted the saddles of lamb turning endlessly on their spits or scrubbed away at the dirty pots.

There were another forty servants—coachmen and grooms—over at the stables, where the horses were led up an inclined roadway to be stabled above the coach-houses which held Bertie's brougham with its dark blue lining, another brougham which Alix used for shopping, a landau, a victoria and others besides.

At this early stage of married life, neither Bertie nor Alix gave much thought to royal duty. They were both too busy enjoying themselves. Alix, when she first found herself deputizing for her mother-in-law at a royal Drawing Room, thought it quite an ordeal. It was as though every lady in London wanted to be among the first to be presented to the new Princess of Wales. More than 3000 of them contrived to secure invitations and their carriages blocked the streets for a mile or more around. So great was the crush that the doors had to be temporarily closed at one point so that Alix, exhausted, could snatch a brief rest. It was nearly six o'clock before the last presentation had been made and the last lady, with her vast crinoline and nodding ostrich plumes, had backed out of the Princess's presence.

The strain of it would perhaps have been too much for any young girl, and Alix, at eighteen, was still little more than a girl and quite unaccustomed to the starchy protocol of such formal occasions. But there were some of those who attended the Drawing Room that day in May who thought they noticed something which neither Queen Victoria nor her daughter, Vicky, for all their intensive investigation into Alix's background and antecedents, had realized until now. Perhaps it had not existed until now. But Alix, at eighteen, was already beginning to suffer from the same deafness which had for so long afflicted her mother. In the years ahead, that disability, becoming worse, was to play its part in encouraging Bertie to seek the company of other women.

But there was, as yet, no thought of other women. He had eyes only for Alix—"Isn't she a pet? Isn't she a darling?"—though a splendid appetite for pleasure—as, indeed, Alix had herself. Nightly they either entertained or were out being entertained. Hardly less lavish than the ball given in their honour by the Brigade of Guards was that given at the Guildhall by the Corporation of the City of London. No pains or expense had been spared to make the indoor setting look as outdoor as possible with a sloping lawn, real flowers and garden paths bathed in a semblance of moonlight. Dominating it all, like a splendid stage setting, was a vast illuminated picture of Alix herself standing before the white-fronted hunting lodge in Denmark where she had spent so many happy childhood hours. Looking at it all, Alix, elegant in a white satin gown surmounted by the glittering £10,000 necklace which had been the City's wedding gift to her, was both enchanted and enchanting.

There was, that year, a visit to Ascot—the first of many—with Alix, in white lace trimmed with mauve ribbons, again contriving to make half-mourning appear both gay and fetching, while Bertie, in a white topper and a jewelled scarf-pin, his race-glasses slung casually across his shoulders, looked every inch the young man-about-town. There was a visit to Cowes—again the first of many; visits to Goodwood. So began a life of carefree, spend-thrift pleasure which Alix, at this early stage of their married life together, enjoyed every bit as much as Bertie.

Of all this, the widowed Queen Victoria, with her narrow, almost puritan, outlook on life, could hardly be expected to approve. Nor did she. Initially she was highly delighted at the apparent change marriage to Alix had wrought in her son. There was "a marked improvement" in him, she wrote to Uncle Leopold in Belgium some two weeks after the wedding; Bertie seemed "really very happy".

But her delight at the change in Bertie soon gave way to disapproval of the sort of runabout life he was leading. "He goes on going out every night until he will become a skeleton", she wrote to Vicky that June. Her regal disapproval quickly widened to include her newly-acquired daughter-in-law as well as her son. The pair of them would soon be "nothing but two puppets running about for show all day and night", she informed Vicky in another letter, written two days before the Brigade of Guards ball.

Concerned as she was, it is perhaps surprising that the Queen did not interfere directly, issuing maternal edicts designed to curtail or prohibit all the running about Bertie and Alix were doing. She was quite capable of doing this over other things of which she did not approve, as she showed later that year.

Alix wanted to go to Rumpenheim to join in the annual holiday get-together of the Hesse-Cassel clan. The Queen promptly put her foot down. Such a journey would be "very imprudent" in Alix's state of health, she said. Alix was then some three months pregnant and it made a good excuse. But there was another reason, as the Queen revealed in a letter to a relative. It would be challenging fate, she felt, to expose Bertie to the obvious temptations of such a gathering.

Instead of going to Rumpenheim, Alix and Bertie holidayed at Abergeldie Castle, a grim-walled structure on the River Dee which Queen Victoria leased from the Gordon family as a guest-house for Balmoral. It was hardly the gayest of holidays. Bertie stalked stag in the hills and helped to net trout on Loch Muick. For Alix, there was only walking—or a drive in a dog-cart to Balmoral to see her mother-in-law.

It was her first glimpse of Balmoral. On the outside, its granite structure, turrets and gables, might look not unlike a Rhineland *schloss*. But inside, she found, it was as Scottish as the traditional kilt, with tartan carpets and curtains, tartan wallpaper, even linoleum in the black, red and lavender Balmoral tartan designed by the Prince Consort and the white-striped Victoria tartan conceived by the Queen herself. Even the lampstands, she noticed, were models of kilted highlanders. She thought it a cold gloomy, cheerless place, smelling of soot and woodsmoke.

After Scotland came another visit to Sandringham. The Great Eastern Line had now been extended to Hunstanton and there was a fine new station at Wolferton which left a carriage drive of only two miles to the house. A train-load of guests and servants travelled with them for their first house-party in their country home.

Compared with some of the house-parties with which Bertie was later to become involved, this one was innocuous in the extreme. Bertie had bought another farm to add to the estate and they walked over to look at it. They drove to Hunstanton, where they climbed down the cliffs, clambered over the rocks and looked at the sea. Bertie went shooting. Alix's pregnancy still showed very little and they hunted with the West Norfolk Foxhounds. Of an evening they and their house-guests played rather childish card games with names like Chow Chow and Fish. On Bertie's birthday, 9th November—he was twenty-two

—they laid on a feast for the men working on the house, the estate workers and the children of the six parishes.

Among their house guests were Vicky, Fritz and little Willy, over from Germany. Vicky thought Sandringham "charming . . . quiet and country-like . . . a delightful house furnished with great taste and comfort."

On 15th November while Alix and Bertie were at Sandringham, word reached them that the childless Frederick of Denmark had died and that Alix's father was the new King. Alix was happy for her father rather than regretful for the death of a monarch she had hardly known and could not resist clapping her hands together in girlish delight.

Suddenly, Prince Christian's hitherto impoverished family was on its way up in the world. Alix was Princess of Wales. The prince himself was now a king. There was also another king in the family—out of the blue, Alix's brother, Willy, a year her junior, suddenly found himself King of the Hellenes.

The uneasy crown of Greece had already been touted round most of the royal courts of Europe. The Duke of Coburg and Prince Leiningen were both offered it and declined. Bertie's brother, Affie, was offered it and Mama quickly declined on his behalf. Alix's brother was even younger than Affie. He accepted with alacrity and was quickly crowned in Athens before he could change his mind.

That December Alix and Bertie went to Windsor to spend Christmas with the Queen. Vicky and Fritz were there too and it should have been a pleasant family occasion. It was very much otherwise. The trouble which had long simmered between Germany and Denmark over Schleswig and Holstein had finally come to the boil . . . and Bertie's wife was daughter of the new King of Denmark while Vicky's husband was son of the Emperor of Prussia.

Things came to a head one evening over dinner. Fritz started it, perhaps without meaning to. The Danes had no claim at all to the two Duchies, he said.

Pregnant though she was, peacemaker though she had always been, Alix was not going to let Fritz get away with that. She spoke up, hotly for her, in her father's defence.

Vicky sided with Fritz; Bertie with Alix. Tempers were close

Sisters and brothers-in-law: (*left*) Vicky and Fritz, the Crown Prince and Princess of Prussia, in the 1870s; (*right*) The Tsarevitch (later Alexander III) and Princess Dagmar at the time of their marriage

Osborne House, 1870: Queen Victoria with two of her children, daughter-in-law Alix and grandchildren Eddy, Georgie and Louise

to being lost and Queen Victoria wished that Albert was back with her to take the children in hand.

She looked round her squabbling family and her mouth tightened.

"Silence," she commanded.

There was a sudden hush round the table.

"None of you will ever mention Schleswig or Holstein in my presence again," the Queen commanded.

PREMATURE BIRTH

The new year of 1864 came in like a lion, hard and cold, with temperatures falling to well below freezing. There was frost on the hedgerows, snow on the ground and ice on the ponds. In so many ways it reminded Alix of her beloved Copenhagen.

She and Bertie were at Frogmore, the damp and rather depressing cream-coloured royal residence in Windsor Great Park which had once been the home of Queen Victoria's mother and it seemed that Alix was taking her first pregnancy very much in her elegant stride. She was in her seventh month and looking extremely well. The baby, according to the physicians' calculations, was not due until mid-March and she and Bertie planned to be back at Marlborough House in good time for the actual confinement.

8th January was yet another day of sharp frost and bright sunshine, with the grass crisp underfoot and the soil beneath it rock-hard. On the pond in front of the house the ice was thicker than ever. It was ideal skating weather.

Alix was up late—unable to match Bertie's long hours and seemingly tireless pace, she was seldom up early—and it was around eleven o'clock when, warmly dressed against the freezing cold, she left Frogmore to drive over to Virginia Water, which for days past had been frozen solid. A few skaters were already out on the ice, the blades of their skates flashing in the morning sunlight, when she arrived. If Alix felt a trifle envious, it was understandable. She loved to skate—her father had taught her when she was still a child—but this winter, because of the baby within her, she had wisely refrained.

She sat now at the edge of the ice in a small sledge, her breath

steaming in the frosty air, watching Bertie take part in a game of
ice hockey. After the game, everyone gathered round a charcoal
fire for the picnic lunch she and Bertie had arranged. It was—as
Bertie's picnics always were—a fairly elaborate affair and Alix
ate, if not enough for two, certainly heartily. Happy and laughing, she was thoroughly enjoying herself and the occasional stab
of pain went almost unnoticed. It was a Dickensian Christmas-
card scene of flushed, happy faces, the ice glinting in the bright
sunlight, and the band of the Blues—the Royal Horse Guards—
playing in the background. Bertie was his customary jovial self.
After lunch, it was back on the ice. Members of a skating club
gave a display in honour of the royal couple, and even Alix,
flushed and laughing, enjoyed the sensation of being propelled
across the ice in her sledge.

But by four o'clock, with dusk closing in, she had had enough.
She was beginning to feel tired, she told Bertie, and thought it
was time she returned to Frogmore. Another pain stabbed her.

With her return to Frogmore, the pains came with increasing
intensity and at increasingly shorter intervals. If Alix and Bertie
were too young and inexperienced to realize at first what was
happening, Alix's motherly lady-in-waiting, Lady Macclesfield,
having herself endured the pangs of childbirth a dozen times, had
little doubt. Either the physicians were seriously out in their
mid-March calculation or something had happened to induce
premature childbirth. Either way, there was not a moment to be
lost.

It was fortunate for Alix that Lady Macclesfield was around to
take charge of things. No one had expected the baby to be born
at Frogmore and nothing was ready. The six celebrated physicians who were to have delivered the baby at Marlborough
House were too far away to be summoned to Frogmore in time.
There was no nurse or midwife in attendance. And no one, as
yet, had given any thought to the question of baby clothes or
linen.

There was certainly no Home Secretary around to witness the
birth of a future heir to the throne in accordance with long-
standing royal custom.

As Alix was seized with another, yet more agonizing pain,
Lady Macclesfield ordered one of the servants to ride post-haste
into Windsor and bring back Dr Brown, the local practitioner.

The doctor arrived, hot and panting, in the nick of time to help with the delivery and was subsequently knighted by Queen Victoria on that account. Between them, these two, the local physician from Windsor and the motherly Lady Macclesfield, with Bertie hovering nervously in the background, brought Alix's first baby into the world, a tiny boy weighing no more than three pounds twelve ounces. It was all over in an hour. Somewhere inside the house, as the baby gave its first worldly cry, a clock chimed. It was nine o'clock.

Delivery had been successfully accomplished. There remained the question of clothes for the baby. Lady Macclesfield again came to the rescue, producing one of her flannel petticoats to serve as a swaddling cloth until proper baby clothes could be bought from a local store in Windsor the following day. The baby slept that night in an improvised nest of cottonwool.

If Alix was tired after the strain of childbirth, Bertie was elated. Tears of joy and excitement in his eyes, he rushed out in search of the Earl of Granville, a Privy Councillor who was staying at Frogmore at the time, bustling him back into the room to serve as official witness to the birth in place of the Home Secretary.

Queen Victoria was at Osborne. As soon as she learned the news she left for Frogmore where she found mother and baby both doing well after the "great danger in such a premature and rapid confinement". Alix, she felt—that "sweet, dear creature"— was "utterly disgusted" by the whole unpleasant business of childbirth. It was "a dear, pretty little baby" whom the Queen hoped would grow up to be "a real grandson of adored Papa".

From Osborne, on her return there, the Queen set about laying down rules and regulations for the baby's christening with all the thoroughness she had displayed earlier in making plans for her son's wedding. She herself would hold the baby at the christening ceremony, she decided. The other sponsors would be Uncle Leopold, Alix's father, Vicky and Aunt Alexandrine, the wife of the dead Prince Consort's elder brother. As for names, the baby must be called after herself and the dead Albert—hence Albert Victor. She did not object to other names, she wrote to the young parents, provided one of them was Uncle Leopold's.

Alix and Bertie had other ideas. Bertie wanted to call the baby Edward. His mother did not agree. That name was better

reserved for a second or third son, she felt. Alix did not see why
King Leopold should be given precedence over her own father.
Finally, parents and grandmother compromised and the baby
was christened Albert Victor Christian Edward. But he was
soon being called Eddy by everyone—including his paternal
grand-mother.

The christening took place at Buckingham Palace on 10th
March—Alix and Bertie's first wedding anniversary. Queen
Victoria thought that Alix, when they met at the ceremony,
looked ill and unhappy. So she did. She was deeply worried and
the fact showed in her young face.

She was worried not about the baby, not about Bertie—who
was still a model husband—but for her parents and her native
Denmark. War had finally broken out between Prussia and
Denmark over the disputed Duchies of Schleswig and Holstein.
Alix worried so much about it that at night she was unable to get
to sleep and more than once Bertie found her weeping bitterly in
the privacy of her bedroom or boudoir.

He felt for her and shared her concern. His mother might
decree that marriage to Alix must be "personal—not political",
but this, to Bertie, was personal in the extreme. Neither he nor
Alix made any secret of how they felt or where their sympathies
lay. Because the Austrians had joined with the Prussians, Alix
refused to meet the new Austrian ambassador. Bertie went about
abusing the Prussians and praising the Danes to an extent which
quite upset his mother (whose sympathies lay with Germany) and
his sister Vicky (whose husband was with the advancing Austro-
Prussian army).

Bertie should remember that he was "bound by so many ties
of blood to Germany and only quite lately, by marriage, to
Denmark", his mother told Lord Clarendon, and he must tone
down his "violent abuse" of Prussia. But Bertie, when
Clarendon spoke to him on the subject, convinced him that his
attitude was both "reasonable and rightminded". Not to have
supported his young wife would be "unfeeling and unnatural",
he said.

Bertie wanted the British fleet to sail into the Baltic in support
of Denmark. When that was ruled out, he offered to go to
Denmark himself to act as an intermediary. His mother would
not permit it.

Bertie tried another tack. If armed intervention was out, Britain should at least try to rescue Denmark by diplomacy, he argued. When Britain finally proposed an armistice, he wrote personally to Alix's father, urging him to accept. His mother, when she heard, ordered him to have no further "political" communication with his father-in-law.

Throughout all this, Bertie still continued to enjoy life. With Alix, he went to race meetings and similar diversions. Night after night they continued to entertain or be entertained. With Alix now seen as the beautiful Danish princess in danger of being devoured by the Prussian dragon, with Bertie as her knight in shining armour, they were more popular than ever—the young, vivacious leaders of London's spendthrift high society.

To Alix's sorrow and Bertie's fury, the war between Germany and Denmark ended the only way it could, with capitulation on Denmark's part and surrender of the Duchies. Alix, as soon as the war was over, wanted to rush off and comfort her parents. It would please them to see the baby, she thought. Bertie said he would go with her.

Queen Victoria promptly forbade it.

But Bertie was beginning to feel his feet and this time he stood up to his mother. Was he a schoolboy, he demanded, who could not be trusted to behave himself?

Finally, the Queen gave way. They could go to Denmark and take baby Eddy with them, but the visit must be strictly personal. Bertie must say nothing rude about Prussia, and they must hold the balance between Denmark and Prussia by going on to see Vicky and Fritz in Berlin.

That September, taking the baby with them, they sailed for Denmark in the *Osborne*. To Alix, after eighteen months of marriage, Denmark was still her home in many ways, though home itself was no longer the small, cosy, barely-furnished Yellow Palace of her childhood, but the larger, grander, if more uncomfortable, Castle of Fredensborg where her parents were now installed as King and Queen. Proudly she showed them their baby grandson. Eagerly she sought the company of her favourite sister. Minnie, now seventeen, had some romantic news to impart. She was to marry Nicholas of Russia, that same Tsarevitch for whom "the horrid Russians", as Vicky called them, had once sought Alix's hand in marriage.

But if Alix was delighted to be again in her native Denmark and overjoyed to be reunited with her parents, Bertie was quickly bored. It was his first visit to Copenhagen and he found it "picturesque", he said. But he also found it dull. Dinner at five o'clock in the afternoon; fruit jelly for every meal; all this talk about other people's ailments—it was all too provincial and boring. He missed the glitter and glamour of London life, the bright, brittle chatter of his society friends. And Alix too, he found, became a different person in the bosom of her own family, as dull as they were. Perhaps marriage too, now that the first romantic blush was wearing off, was beginning to pall. Bertie craved life and excitement, not all this sitting around talking about baby Eddy and Minnie's marriage prospects. While Alix stayed with her parents, he took off on his own on a trip to Stockholm, where he went elk-hunting with the King of Sweden and flirted with some pretty girls.

From Copenhagen, Bertie and Alix went on to Hanover and Hesse, where they met Alice and Louis. But they did not go to Berlin, as Queen Victoria had ordained. That would have meant calling on the Queen of Prussia and this Alix refused to do.

With Alix, Prussia's treatment of Denmark had gone deep. She never forgot what had happened and it was to be a long time before she forgave. When Prince Charles of Prussia visited England the following year, she turned her head away when he was presented to her. And three years later, at Wiesbaden, she was still refusing to see the King of Prussia when he wanted to call on her. She was in mourning, she said—then gave the lie to her words by going out into the public gardens to listen to the band.

So instead of going to Berlin, Bertie and Alix met Vicky and Fritz on Cologne railway station. The meeting was brief and lacking in family warmth. Fritz was in army uniform and wearing a decoration awarded to him for the campaign against Denmark.

"A most objectionable ribbon," Bertie sniffed, contemp-tuously.

"IT GETS WORSE INSTEAD OF BETTER"

It was 1865 and Alix was again pregnant. Her deafness was not yet such as to spoil the pleasure of music for her and on the afternoon of 2nd June she went to a concert given by the orchestra which Sir Charles Hallé, the noted conductor and pianist, had formed some six years earlier. She enjoyed the concert, but by the time she returned to Marlborough House she was feeling—as she had felt at Virginia Water some seventeen months earlier—very tired.

She excused herself from playing hostess at a small dinner party Bertie was giving that evening and went to bed. But not to sleep. At one o'clock the following morning her second child was born, another son.

It was, it seemed, another premature birth. Or was it? Eddy, as his weight at birth showed, had been clearly premature. But the second baby was nicely plump and there were some who whispered that Alix and Bertie had deliberately misled everyone in order to prevent Bertie's mother moving in and taking charge of things in her fussy, autocratic fashion.

If Queen Victoria was at all disappointed in this, she concealed her disappointment well. "I am glad I am spared the anxiety and fatigue of being with Alix at this time," she wrote to Uncle Leopold in Brussels, "though I should never shun it."

But she again interfered when it came to names for the new baby. Bertie and Alix wanted to call him George. "We like the name and it is English," Bertie informed his mother.

The Queen didn't very much care for the name. But more and more, Bertie and Alix were learning that if they stuck out, Mama gave in. "We are sorry to hear that you don't like the names we are giving our little boy," Bertie wrote to her, "but they are names that we like and have decided upon for some time."

"Of course you will add Albert at the end," the Queen wrote back from her Highland fastness at Balmoral. "We settled long ago that all dearest Papa's male descendants should bear that name."

The baby was accordingly christened George Frederick Ernest Albert.

Alix did not feed the baby herself. She hired a 'wet nurse' to
perform the task for her. But she was often in the nursery,
washing and dressing and playing with her two small sons.

She was with them the day Bertie burst suddenly into the
nursery with news that the house was on fire. There was, as it
happened, no real danger and to Bertie himself the incident was a
welcome and exciting break in the tedium of everyday life. He
hustled Alix and the children to safety, ordered the fire hose run
out, organized the servants into a human chain to fight the
outbreak with buckets and jugs of water.

The smoke was thickest near the nursery. Bertie seized an axe
and began ripping up the floorboards, hacking at them so furiously that he nearly fell through the rafters into the room
below.

By now, the fire hose had been run out. Face blackened, his
clothes covered in dust, Bertie proceeded to pour water on the
fire with such abandon that he also sent a cascade streaming down
the stairs.

Captain Shaw of the London Fire Brigade was coming up the
stairs at the time. "What's all this mess?" he wanted to know.

Bertie enjoyed the whole affair so much that he asked Shaw to
keep him informed of any future big blaze in London. He would
go along and lend a hand, he said—and soon after he was among
the fire-fighters who tackled the blaze at the El Dorado music
hall in Leicester Square.

Both Bertie and Alix still harboured bitter memories of
Prussia's attack on Denmark. Now fresh fuel was fed to the
flames of their bitterness with the news that Lenchen, Bertie's
sister, was to marry Prince Christian, brother of the Duke of
Augustenburg whose claim to Schleswig and Holstein had
helped precipitate the Prussian attack.

"Bertie and Alix will be much annoyed," Queen Victoria
prophesied.

They were, indeed. They went so far as to threaten to stay
away from the wedding. Bertie's other sister, Alice, wrote to
him, urging them to do nothing so drastic. Mama, said Alice,
had not allowed political considerations to stand in the way of his
marriage to Alix. It was only fair that he and Alix should not let
political considerations stand in the way of Lenchen's happiness.

In the end they gave way and, however reluctantly, attended the wedding at Windsor in the July of the following year.

All this family upset, of course, did nothing to commend them to the Queen. She was inclined to blame Alix rather than Bertie, and perhaps she was right.

"She is grown a little grand," the Queen complained of her daughter-in-law. She was not a proper Princess; she was unsympathetic.

The Queen, at this time and for some time to come, was highly displeased with her Danish daughter-in-law. Alix was no longer the "dear, sweet child" . . . the jewel". She could, it seemed, do nothing right—at least, in the Queen's eyes. Even her hunting with the West Norfolk Foxhounds during visits to Sandringham came in for regal disapproval. Her hunting must stop, the Queen ordered.

Eager to make peace with her mother-in-law, anxious to restore the old warm relationship between the two of them, Alix did stop hunting—for a time. But, later, she again followed the hounds.

For her and Bertie, life went on as gaily and excitingly as ever, a seemingly endless succession of race meetings, house parties, dinners and balls. Bertie showed not the slightest sign that he would ever tire of this never-ending round of pleasure. If Alix was tiring of it, she kept it to herself. She loved Bertie and was happy to do whatever he wanted. But, physically, she was less able to conceal the fatigue that sometimes crept over her.

She had sometimes good reason to feel fatigued. Their private parties at Marlborough House went on, usually, until the first fingers of a new day crept over the rooftops of Victorian London. They were gay, lively parties, with the carpets rolled back for dancing, ending, as often as not, in hilarious, almost childish, practical jokes which Alix enjoyed every bit as much as Bertie, and sometimes in out-and-out horseplay. The young men would come sliding down the stairs on trays or would start squirting each other with soda syphons, a recently invented novelty. Alix, on one occasion at least, proved herself no mean shot with a soda syphon.

Bertie, however energetically he pranced and danced at night, whatever time he went to bed, was always up and about in good time the following morning. Alix, more easily tired, physically less resilient, would lie late abed. No longer did they breakfast together as in the early months of marriage. While Alix still slept, Bertie, after a brisk early-morning stroll in St James's or Green Park, would breakfast alone in his walnut-panelled sitting room looking out on the clubs of Pall Mall, the faint skirl of pipes reaching him from the piper parading up and down in the garden outside. Alix, when she finally stirred, would similarly breakfast alone in either her sitting room or her boudoir.

This state of affairs worried Queen Victoria when she heard of it. At loggerheads with her daughter-in-law, she was inclined to blame Alix rather than Bertie.

"I am sorry for Bertie," she wrote to Vicky, and went on to give her reasons. Alix did not make Bertie's home comfortable. She was never ready for breakfast and often not out of bed until eleven.

"I think it gets much worse instead of better," the Queen lamented. "It makes me unhappy and anxious."

PART THREE

The Widening Gulf

"WILL IT NEVER GET BETTER?"

As summer gave way to autumn in the year 1866 Alix was again pregnant. Whether or not she found the business of childbirth "disgusting", as Queen Victoria judged, she must have felt that she was nearly always preparing for it or recovering from it. In less than four years of marriage this was her third pregnancy. Nor was it proving so easy as the first two. She had carried her first two children easily enough and the long months of pregnancy had interfered little with the round of pleasure she enjoyed with Bertie. But almost from the outset, this third pregnancy was tedious and frustrating—different.

She was frustrated by the fact that she was in no condition to undertake the long and tiring journey to St Petersburg, where the dark-eyed and dark-haired Minnie, the sister to whom she was so close, was to marry the Tsarevitch of Russia, though not the same young Tsarevitch about whom she had whispered so excitedly to Alix when the two of them were last together. That was Nicholas, who, sadly, had since died of tuberculosis. But the Russians, having lost Alix to Bertie, were determined not to lose her sister. Nicholas might be dead, but his brother Alexander was alive and well, the new Tsarevitch and future Emperor. He needed a wife and Russia a future Empress. So now the vivacious, chatterbox Minnie was to marry Alexander, six feet four inches tall and so strong, it was said, he could tie a knot in a silver fork and bend a poker with his bare hands.

But Alix, though she could not go to St Petersburg herself, agreed that Bertie should go. Minnie wanted him there—there would be so few relatives from her side, she wrote—and he wanted to go. As restless as ever, with no worthwhile job of work to occupy his time, he found it tedious and boring to be tied to the side of a pregnant wife. So while Alix took the children—Eddy, now approaching his third birthday, and the toddling Georgie—to stay with Gan-gan at Windsor, a handsomely-bearded Bertie set off to sample the delights of St Petersburg.

The marriage ceremony in the chapel of the vast Winter Palace on 9th November—coincidentally Bertie's twenty-fifth birthday—lasted only a few minutes. To be there for those few minutes Bertie was gone six weeks. He returned to find Alix ailing from something more than mere pregnancy. Her whole body seemed to ache. One leg and hip were especially painful. Racked with pain, she tossed and turned fitfully at night, unable to sleep.

With the children, they went to Sandringham for Christmas. It rained torrents and the whole house seemed to smell of damp. Alix returned to London worse than before and the physicians attending her diagnosed acute rheumatism. Their third child, a daughter, was born—again prematurely—on 20th February 1867. Two days before, an official bulletin concerning Alix's state of health had been posted outside Marlborough House. There was no cause for anxiety, it said. Perhaps not, but the people of Britain had taken Alix to their hearts from the first moment she set foot in the country. Now they wanted to help and Marlborough House was inundated with cure-alls of all kinds. Alix was deeply touched by this show of public affection. But neither the cure-alls nor the physicians seemed capable of effecting any immediate cure. Long after the actual ordeal of childbirth was over Alix remained feverish and in pain. Sometimes the pain was so bad that she had to be given chloroform.

Worried about her, sympathetic and understanding at first, wanting to be with her as much as possible, Bertie had his desk moved into her bedroom so that he could work at the bedside, chatting to her between letter-writing. But there was little work of real consequence to occupy him and his was not a nature to sit contentedly for long at anyone's sickbed. Increasingly, he became bored and restless.

His mother may have exaggerated when she said that he was interested only in clothes. But, certainly, they were among his main pre-occupations. He was constantly buying new clothes and soon had so many that it required two valets and a brusher to keep them spruce. As fastidious as any woman, he would change up to half-a-dozen times a day and boasted that he could make a complete change of outfit in ten minutes flat.

But he was interested also in entertaining and being entertained, in racing and gambling, and, increasingly, in beautiful
women. He was unwise in his choice of friends, surrounding
himself, then and later, with beautiful, brash young women and
wild, dissolute young men. His mother disapproved of his choice
of friends. To her, the goings-on among some English aristocrats
was not unlike what had happened in France in the days prior to
the Revolution. With some exceptions, she wrote to Vicky, the
aristocracy were "frivolous, pleasure-seeking, heartless, selfish
and immoral". The young men were "ignorant, luxurious and
self-indulgent"; the young women "fast, frivolous and imprudent". They lived only to "kill time" and Bertie ought not to
countenance such "horrid people".

Bertie did more than countenance them. He made bosom
friends of some . . . among them Lord Hartington, who slept in
turn with Lottie, wife of the Duke of Manchester, and the
chestnut-haired 'Skittles' Walters, one of London's most notorious prostitutes; Sir Frederick Johnstone, who was to be cited in
the Mordaunt divorce case; Colonel Valentine Baker, who was
sent to prison for his over-amorous approaches to a young
woman who found herself alone in a railway carriage with him;
and the Marquis of Hastings, who eloped with Lady Florence
Paget when the date was already set for her marriage to Harry
(later Viscount) Chaplin.

It was in company with Hastings, a wild, headstrong young
man that Bertie, while Alix was ill, first tasted the pleasures of
London's night life. Together, they went to cock fights and prize
fights, music halls and dance halls, baccarat clubs and 'night
houses'. They explored Regent Street and the Haymarket, with
their hordes of prostitutes, and visited Cremorne Gardens in
Chelsea, strolling cloaked and silk-hatted under the Chinese
lanterns among the prostitutes and semi-professional 'dolly
mops'—housemaids, shop girls and young wives craving
excitement—in their saucy bonnets and brightly-coloured shawls.

Whether Bertie was unfaithful to Alix on these excursions
there is no way of knowing. Perhaps, at this stage, he sought
stimulation rather than indulgence. He was both over-sexed and
emotionally immature, with a passion, which Alix shared, for
schoolboyish practical jokes. Bertie's idea of a good joke was to
tuck a dead seagull into bed with a friend who had retired the

worse for drink. He found it great fun, too, to pour a glass of brandy over the head of the obsequious Christopher Sykes, listening to his whining "As Your Royal Highness pleases" while the brandy trickled down his face and into his beard. Bertie, as his mother said in an earlier letter to Vicky, was inclined to tyrannize those, like Sykes, who were weak and admire those, like Hastings, who did not 'knock under' so easily.

Whether or not he was physically unfaithful, he was certainly inconsiderate and disloyal. Night after night, while Alix tossed and turned in her bed, unable to sleep for the pain in her hip and leg, he was rampaging about London. In vain, Alix's nurse tried to persuade her to take the drugs which would induce sleep. She must be awake when Bertie got back, Alix insisted; she must know he was safely home. Some nights it was two or three in the morning before he came in and only then could Alix be persuaded to settle down.

While Bertie was increasingly disloyal and perhaps unfaithful, Alix was constancy itself. Whatever she may have known or suspected, she kept it to herself. Bertie's friends were her friends. Lottie, Duchess of Manchester, Lord Hartington's mistress, was perhaps her closest friend. From her, or someone else, Alix must have learned—something. Her hearing may have been affected, but, as Queen Victoria said when gossip concerning Bertie's indiscretions reached her own ears, Alix was "not blind".

Illness and worry pulled into her. Queen Victoria, making a special journey from Windsor to visit her, was horrified by her condition. She was tossing and turning in pain, unable to eat because of the condition of her throat, exhausted from lack of sleep.

The Queen was quickly touched, as always, by the sight of anyone in pain or distress. Past irritations with her daughter-in-law forgotten, she sat by the bedside and cradled Alix's head on her shoulder.

"Will it never get better?" Alix asked, despairingly.

It was to be a long time before she turned the corner and her illness was to leave a legacy of lameness and increasing deafness which would be with her for the rest of her life. She was so ill that her mother travelled from Denmark to look after her. Her father came a day or two later. It was mid-April, with the trees in the Marlborough House garden bursting into the fresh green

(*Left*) Princesses Victoria, Maud and Louise; (*below*) Eddy and Georgie as cadets in 1877

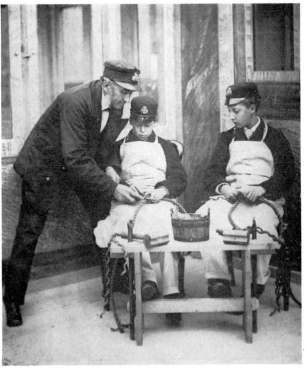

Alix and her children

of a new spring, before Alix showed signs of improvement and it was May before she was well enough to be wheeled from her bedroom to the drawing room for the christening of her third child. The Queen wanted the baby called Victoria after herself. Alix thought her own mother should come first. The baby was accordingly christened Louise Victoria Alexandra Dagmar.

Later that same day Bertie said goodbye and, with Affie in tow, took off for Paris.

PARIS

Paris in 1867 . . . the Paris of the Second Empire . . . a gay, gaudy, brash, brittle city where life was like a perpetual cancan danced to the brassy strains of Offenbach's music. A city of extravagant pleasure and easy money which attracted adventurers and whores from all parts of France, from all over Europe. The Paris of Hortense Schneider, as notorious for her lovers as she was famous for her singing. The Paris of Sarah Bernhardt, the actress, another woman of many loves and many lovers. The Paris of the courtesans—Cora Pearl, who was born one of eleven children of an impoverished music-teacher in Plymouth and now lived in a mansion which cost £80,000; Therese Lachmann, the bright-eyed, sensual Russian Jewess who married the Marquis de Paiva for his title and deserted him almost immediately for a succession of wealthy lovers; Giulia Beneni, the dark-eyed, golden-skinned Italian beauty whose jewels were said to be worth a million francs; Leonide Leblanc, the labourer's daughter who arrived barefoot in Paris and now had a fortune in diamonds and pearls; and many more whose beautiful, amoral bodies were their passports to wealth and notoriety.

Bertie had gone to Paris ostensibly to open the British section of the Great Exhibition. The Duc de Grammont-Caderousse and the Duc de Mouchy became his guides to the city of pleasure. Two of the biggest roués in France, they were hardly the most suitable companions for a young man of Bertie's inclination and temperament. With them, he visited artists' studios, back-stage dressing rooms, dance rehearsals, all places where there were attractive, exciting, scantily-clad women to be seen. He saw Hortense Schneider at the Variétés and went back-stage to pay

court to her in her dressing room. He watched the girls of the
Opera House at their exercises in the foyer de danse. At the
Jardin Mabille he revelled in the high-kicking abandonment of
the cancan. At supper parties in private rooms at the Café
Anglais and Maison D'Or, he rubbed shoulders with notorious
courtesans.

If he did not join the circle of male admirers who clustered
round Cora Pearl as she reclined naked on the sofa in her
boudoir, there was a night when he was among those present
at the Café Anglais when Cora staged one of her favourite
divertissements . . . having herself served as the main dish of the
evening, nude or nearly nude, on a huge silver platter. There was
an equally stimulating encounter with Giulia Beneni, who everyone knew was "the biggest sinner in Paris".

Beneni's late arrival at a supper party held in the Maison D'Or
created a considerable sensation. She was wearing a diaphanous
gown designed to reveal rather than conceal her physical charms.

The Duc de Grammont-Caderousse presented her to Bertie.
The Prince of Wales must forgive her late arrival, he said; she
was the most unpunctual woman in all France.

"Now behave yourself and show His Royal Highness your
best side," the Duc admonished her, jokingly.

Beneni did so, turning and flipping up the diaphanous dress to
display the shapely buttocks beneath.

"My best side," she said, coquettishly.

Rumours of Bertie's adventures in Paris filtered back to
Mama in England.

"Our poor boy . . . has the best intentions, but is not discreet,"
the Queen lamented to Lord Clarendon.

By the time Bertie returned home Alix was much improved.
But not fully recovered. Nor was she ever to recover entirely.
Queen Victoria, visiting her again, found her "altered" and
wrote to Vicky that Alix would "never be what she was". Illness
had left her with a leg and hip so stiff as to amount almost to
lameness and in the aftermath of her illness she was increasingly
aware of the handicap of deafness. It was a terrible double burden
to be borne by a young woman not yet twenty-three.

There was hope that the waters at Wiesbaden, one of Europe's
most fashionable spas, might work some sort of a miracle and
Bertie took her there. Along with their three children and a small

army of servants, they sailed from Woolwich on the *Osborne*. Included in their luggage was a specially-made chair in which Alix could be carried around.

Illness had left her painfully thin and fragile looking, yet still beautiful as a Dresden figure is beautiful. But beauty alone was never enough to hold Bertie.

To Alix's disappointment, he was quickly bored with the peace and quiet of Wiesbaden, quickly tired of keeping his pace down to the painful hobble she could just about manage with the aid of sticks. Leaving her to take the waters on her own, he nipped off to Baden, the summer capital of Europe. To Baden each summer flocked the cream of Paris society, and the attendant *demi-mondaines*. At Baden there was racing, gambling, the company of beautiful women, and once again gossip concerning his indiscretions drifted back to Queen Victoria.

The waters at Wiesbaden did little, if anything, to improve the condition of Alix's leg. It was still stiff, sometimes painful, and she returned home still walking with the aid of sticks. Getting up and down stairs or in and out of carriages was particularly awkward for her.

There had been a moment of weakness during her long illness when she had asked her mother-in-law, "Will it never get better?" But now she bore her affliction with almost stoic-like patience, and the stay in Wiesbaden, if it did little to ease her leg, did much to improve her general health and raise her spirits. She arrived back home determined to make the best of things.

In the years which lay ahead she was to fight as bravely as a woman can in her efforts to hold her husband, to be the same bright, beautiful creature he had married, to match up to his own restless, pleasure-seeking nature. Married to a man like Bertie, she could not hope to win, but she never gave up trying, never—or hardly ever—despaired.

Becoming more accustomed to the stiffness of her leg, she took up dancing again, her long skirts masking her lameness though they did nothing to ease the discomfort she felt. She took up riding and hunting again. She had a special saddle made so that she could sit her mares, Victoria and Viva, on the reverse side. It was never easy for her and sometimes dangerous. There was one occasion, out hunting, when her mount bolted. The old Alix, experienced horsewoman that she was, would have handled the runaway with comparative ease. But incapacitated by her leg, she could not keep her seat in the saddle. Her foot trapped in the stirrup, her hands still clutching the reins, her head was only just clear of the ground as the runaway raced along. Only quick thinking and quick action on the part of Sir Dighton Probyn, who was with her, saved her from a serious accident. Galloping in pursuit, he overtook her, grabbed the bridle and forced her runaway mount to a standstill.

Whether dancing or hunting, inevitably she tired more easily. No longer could she match up to Bertie's seemingly inexhaustible pursuit of pleasure. And perhaps she no longer had any real desire to do so. More and more they drifted apart. Her worsening deafness did nothing to help, and Bertie became increasingly bored with a wife with whom it was difficult even to hold a proper conversation.

One of her doctors had the idea that her illness might have been brought about by exposure to damp. Frogmore, where she had had her first child, was notorious for its dampness. Sandringham, where she and Bertie continued to spend much of their time, was equally damp—so damp that in the servants' quarters water streamed down the walls in wet weather.

Alterations and improvements to Sandringham had already cost Bertie a small fortune. Further land had been bought to enlarge the estate, though more to add to its shooting potential than for any farming Bertie proposed to do. A new high wall of red-brown sandstone now encircled the park to make for added privacy. The old conservatory had been turned into a billiards room. Most of Bertie's cronies were adept at the game and he was taking lessons from one of the country's top players. A bowling alley had also been built on, together with a new wing for the servants.

All this had cost a packet of money. Indeed, Bertie's entire pleasure-seeking way of life cost money and year after year his outgoings contrived to exceed his income.

Despite all he had already spent on Sandringham, concerned for Alix despite his increasing unfaithfulness, Bertie came to a big decision. He would tear the whole place down and build it afresh from scratch, free (he hoped) from damp. Demolition and rebuilding were to take the best part of two years and cost him another small fortune.

"A VERY DISSOLUTE LIFE"

Alix sat in her room at Marlborough House, penning a letter to her royal mother-in-law, Queen Victoria. Bertie was going to Ireland and more than anything she wanted to go with him.

She was still not well enough, Bertie had said.

But Alix, though still in pain from her hip and again pregnant, was determined to go.

Hers was not the determination of a jealous wife who cannot bear to let her husband out of her sight. Rather was it the anxiety and loyalty of a still loving wife who fears for her husband's safety. Fenianism was on the upsurge and already Bertie's younger brother, Affie, had been shot in the back, seriously though not fatally wounded, by a Fenian sympathizer at a charity picnic in Australia. For Bertie, as Prince of Wales, there was a considerable risk in going to Ireland and Alix wanted to share the risk with him.

She said nothing of this to Bertie. Instead, she wrote secretly to his mother. The Queen understood her daughter-in-law's wish to be with her husband. Perhaps she also hoped that Alix's presence would serve as something of a check on Bertie's constant love of running about. Either way, she gave her royal permission and Alix was at Bertie's side when he arrived in Kingstown on 15th April 1868.

For her, that nine-day visit to Ireland was to prove a considerable ordeal. She was some six months' pregnant. Her leg still troubled her and she frequently needed the aid of sticks when she walked.

Yet, with Bertie, she visited hospitals and orphanages, schools and police barracks. She was with him when he was installed as a Knight of St Patrick in the cathedral; beside him during a military review at Phoenix Park where he unveiled a statue of Edmund Burke. She even took part in the square dancing during a ball at the Mansion House in Dublin.

Between them, Bertie and Alix completely charmed the Irish. Bertie, prematurely balding like his father before him, wore a shamrock-green tie for the Punchestown Races which he attended despite his mother's disapproval. Alix wore one Irish fashion after another . . . a gown of green Irish poplin, a white bonnet trimmed with shamrock, an evening shawl of Irish lace. The Irish loved her for it. They whispered among themselves that she had a magic touch and had charmed away the warts which plagued the hands of the Viceroy's eight-year-old son.

Queen Victoria, though she had given way to Alix and let her go to Ireland with Bertie, was worried as to the effect the trip might have on the baby Alix was carrying. She feared it would be born like all the rest, "such miserable puny little children (each weaker than the preceding one) . . . poor frail little fairies". Mother-in-law like, she exaggerated somewhat. Georgie, at least, was growing up strong and robust.

Bertie and Alix had been back from Ireland six weeks when Alix, on her own, drove out to the Crystal Palace to attend a gala concert given by Adelina Patti, the celebrated opera singer. The following day—6th July 1868—she gave birth to her fourth child, another daughter. This time she gave way to her mother-in-law and named the baby after her—Victoria Alexandra Olga Marie.

Alix now had the comfort and childish companionship of four children around her. She needed all the comfort she could get as Bertie continued to gallivant around as indiscreetly as ever. He was away from home at all hours of the day and night. By night he continued to explore the seamier strands of London life. By day, hopping into a hired hansom instead of using his own more easily recognized brougham, he made calls upon various young women of his acquaintance. Some, like Harriet Mordaunt, were married. But one, Catherine Walters, was unmarried.

Catherine Walters, whom her lovers knew as Skittles and sometimes Skitsie, was two years older than Bertie. With a mass of chestnut hair and wide, appealing, blue-grey eyes, she combined an air of almost childish innocence with an abounding and lusty sensuality. To men, it was an almost irresistible combination and Catherine Walters, from her early teens, was not slow to capitalize upon it. She first burst upon the London scene as one of what the Victorians, with their knack for calling sordid things by attractive names, referred to as "the pretty little horsebreakers of Hyde Park". It was a synonym for a classy type of prostitute. Clad in a close-fitting riding habit which served to accentuate rather than conceal her physical charms, a cherry-red ribbon fastened prettily about her throat, Skittles cantered round the park on a hired hack—until one of Bertie's friends, Lord Hartington, provided her with both a house and horse of her own. He also made her his mistress, a fact which caused Bertie to remark that she was far to good for a dullard like Harty-Tarty.

When Hartington tired of her and returned to his old love, Lottie, Duchess of Manchester, Catherine Walters took off for Paris. There, she became the mistress of Achille Fould, financial adviser to the Emperor Napoleon. Now, a few years and several men later, she was a notorious success in her chosen field, wealthy enough to divide her time between Paris, where she drove along the Avenue de l'Imperatrice in a carriage drawn by gleaming thoroughbreds with two liveried grooms on horseback in attendance, London, where she had a house in Mayfair, and Leicestershire, where she hunted with the Quorn. Bertie had seen her with Harty-Tarty, run across her briefly in Paris and now, staying at the Melton Mowbray home of Sir Frederick Johnstone, who also hunted with the Quorn, he met her again. There was something in Bertie that was always drawn irresistibly to women who were sensual and brash as well as beautiful—and Catherine Walters, with her child's face and woman's body, was undeniably all three.

Bertie took to calling upon her in London, and just as Nellie Clifden had been unable to keep her pretty little mouth shut about what had happened on the Curragh, so Catherine Walters was unable to resist boasting of her latest conquest. But, curiously, she did not boast of it in sexual terms. She whispered instead that she served as a go-between for the Prince of Wales and Gladstone, who was now prime minister. There may or may not have been truth in that, but certainly Gladstone from time to time also called upon Catherine at her house with its gilt and crimson decor borrowed from the Second Empire.

It was not long since Queen Victoria had lamented that Bertie was "not discreet". Now he became increasingly obvious. His French friends, the Duc de Grammont-Caderousse and the Duc du Mouchy, carried on their infidelities in Paris quite openly and he saw no reason why he should not do the same in London. As his private life became more and more public property, as there was more and more gossip about his wild ways, there was a degree of alarm in high places. He was not only leading "a very dissolute life", said Lord Clarendon, but "far from concealing it, his wish seems to be to earn himself the reputation of a roué".

THE MAN WHO LOVED ALIX

Alix too, was distressed about Bertie's wild and dissolute way of life. Later she was to become more reconciled to his goings-on. But not yet. Loving him as she did (and as she would always love him), she still hoped to win him back and have him again to herself. So she made all manner of excuses to herself for the way he treated her. She blamed his friends for putting temptation in his way. To her, as to his mother, he was "poor Bertie", to be pitied rather than blamed.

She did not fly into jealous rages with him, as some wives would have done. She did not attempt to pay him back in his own coin, though she was, despite her ill-health, attractive enough to have done so. She did not go running to her royal mother-in-law with demands that Bertie should toe the line of marital fidelity. She did not pour out her troubles to those around.

Of those close to her, perhaps only one sensed the true depth of her unhappiness at this time of ill-health, wounded pride and lost love. The Hon. Oliver Montagu, younger son of the Earl of Sandwich and an officer in the Blues, had recently been appointed as one of Bertie's equerries, a position in which he was soon perhaps to know more of Bertie's extra-marital adventures than Alix did herself. And knowing, he felt both pity for her and admiration for the proud way she conducted herself.

Like Bertie's younger brother, Affie, the unmarried Montagu was strongly attracted to Alix's cool, aloof beauty from the first moment he saw her. For nearly a quarter of a century, from his appointment in 1868 to his death in 1893, he was constantly at her side. He was quickly devoted to her and what started as devotion soon turned to something very akin to love. But it was not the sort of 'love' Bertie felt for the brash, loose young women he pursued so insatiably. It was something deeper, finer.

If Alix knew how Montagu felt towards her (and she could

hardly not have known), she gave no outward sign. The only physical contact between them was when he held her, distantly after the fashion of the day, as they danced together. It became an unspoken arrangement between them for her always to save him the first after-supper waltz. And his feeling for her was revealed only in a single unguarded phrase in a letter he once wrote to a close relative, or perhaps by the look in his eyes when he was in her company. That was as far as it ever went, as far as Montagu dare let it go, and, almost certainly, as far as Alix wanted it to go. She needed a show of affection and understanding from someone, but nothing more. With all his faults, she still loved only Bertie.

If only, she thought, she could wean him right away from his current circle of unsuitable friends, get him right away from temptation for a time, she might yet win him back and bring the two of them again as close together as they were in the early days of marriage.

The children were growing up. Eddy was still a pale and sickly child as he approached his fifth birthday, but Georgie, some eighteen months younger, was a sturdy little chap with rosy cheeks. Little Louise was perhaps small for her age. The baby, Victoria, was small too, but plump with it. Alix suggested that they should take the children to visit Amama and Apapa in Copenhagen. And why not go to Greece as well? It was a long time since she had seen her brother Willy, the King of the Hellenes.

To her surprise, Bertie hailed the idea with enthusiasm. He, too, felt the need to get away for a time, particularly from the strongly outspoken attacks being made on him by freethinker Charles Bradlaugh and others. Bertie should "never dishonour this country by becoming its King", Bradlaugh had said.

Between them, he and Alix worked out plans for a long trip which would include a visit to Napoleon and the Empress Eugénie, then on to Denmark so that Alix's parents could see their four grandchildren, Berlin to see Vicky and Fritz, Austria, Egypt, Turkey, and finally a stop-over in Greece to see Alix's brother and his teenage bride, the Grand Duchess Olga, niece of Tsar Alexander II.

Planning was one thing. Getting Mama's permission was quite another. The Queen, as always, laid down rules and regulations.

They must travel incognito as Lord and Lady Renfrew instead of the Prince and Princess of Wales. They could take only Eddy and Georgie to Denmark with them; not the two girls. They were still too young for such a journey.

Her mother-in-law's edict concerning the children upset Alix. She wanted her parents to see all their grandchildren, she told Bertie. Unfaithful though he was, disloyal to her in so many ways, Bertie, in this at least, was an understanding and sympathetic husband. Realizing how much it meant to Alix to take all the children to Denmark, he proceeded to do battle with his mother on her behalf. The Queen was obstinate. So, for once, was Alix. Bertie, caught in the middle, finally achieved a compromise between his mother and wife. They could take the three older children to Denmark with them, but not Toria, still a baby of only a few months. And they would send the other children home from Denmark to stay with Gan-gan, before embarking on the rest of the trip.

Not that Queen Victoria, as she confided in Vicky, wanted her house crammed full of so many children for so long. "But I think it is so important that they should be well looked after (which they are not)".

Alix and Bertie might be travelling incognito, as Queen Victoria had ordained, but the usual small army of officials and servants went with them. Among them was Oliver Montagu.

They went first to Compiègne to stay with Napoleon and Eugénie. Then on to Fredensborg where the children, all except the baby Victoria, joined them for Christmas. It was a real family get-together. Minnie and her husband, the tall, amiable Sasha had travelled from St Petersburg to be there too. In the bosom of her family, reunited with her favourite sister, Alix thoroughly enjoyed herself, her troubles forgotten for a time at least. But Bertie found the family atmosphere of his Danish in-laws dull after London and again shot off on his own to sample the livelier pleasures of Stockholm.

Christmas over, the children were packed off to stay with Gan-gan, while Alix and Bertie went on to Berlin to see Vicky and Fritz. Next stop was Vienna which they reached after a long, tiring journey through the biting cold of the European winter. They stayed in Vienna for six days of banquets and balls, opera and concerts, skating and sightseeing before going on to Trieste, where the frigate *Ariadne*, specially fitted out to serve as a royal yacht, was waiting to take them to Egypt.

Bertie had been to Egypt before, but this was Alix's first visit. To her, it was all new and strange, colourful and exotic—the dark-skinned Arabs in their bright robes, the processions of pilgrims, the women of the harem—and she enjoyed it in childlike, open-mouthed fashion. She returned from visiting the harem wearing the robe and yashmak of a female slave. There was a six-week, 900-mile trip up the Nile in a blue-and-gold boat, panelled in mother-of-pearl, which had been named *Alexandra* in Alix's honour. Bertie shot a crocodile and Alix, whose heart could always rule her head, adopted a Nubian waif who she brought back to England with her and had christened at Sandringham.

As the long holiday ran its course, her general health seemed quite restored and even her lame leg seemed much improved. She walked everywhere, seemingly tireless. Bertie, increasing plumpness betraying his love of good living, often tired more easily than she did.

They crossed from Egypt to Turkey and then went on to Greece to see Willy. It was their first meeting with his teenage wife and their first glimpse of their two babies, Tino and George.

They returned home by way of Paris where a letter from Queen Victoria awaited them.

"The dear little children are very well . . . and are very fond of Grandmama." The Queen went on to give advice about the future upbringing of her grandchildren. They should be made to keep regular hours; to get up early and go to bed in good time. They should not be allowed downstairs with their parents for too long at a time and not all together. "One at a time is much the best."

It was early May when Alix and Bertie got back to Marlborough House. Both were pleased to be home and see the children again. Alix, in particular, had missed the children at times. She enjoyed having them around her again, all of them, all at once, despite Queen Victoria's admonition. She was, indeed, almost inseparable from them, taking them for drives in her carriage, putting on a flannel apron to bath them at night, insisting on putting them to bed herself. Eddy, by now, was showing signs of the delicate, poetically-handsome good looks he was to display later. But there was also, even if Alix did not notice, something a bit odd—dreamy—about him. He was his mother's favourite, perhaps because he was her firstborn, perhaps because he seemed always so delicate, and George, his brother, was sometimes hurt at the way she seemed to favour Eddy.

Bertie, too, his restlessness appeased for a time, revelled in the company of the children, happy to have them play around him as he sat in his study, writing letters. The long trip he and Alix had undertaken together had done—or seemed to have done— what it was intended to do. They were, for a time, again as close to each other as they had been in the early days of marriage and their new-found closeness was cemented by the knowledge that another baby was on the way.

But if Alix deluded herself that things would stay this way, Bertie's mother did not. From a distance, she saw, perhaps more clearly than they did themselves, the gulf that yawned between them; how dissimilar and unsuited they were in so many ways. Alix might love Bertie with all her heart, but she could never, as Queen Victoria realized, hope to hold him. She was not his type of woman, and his mother, thinking back, was sometimes regretful that she had picked Alix as Bertie's bride. Elizabeth of Wied, the way things had turned out, would perhaps have suited him better, she confided to Vicky. "He wants a cleverer and better-informed wife to amuse and occupy him."

That autumn, Alix, well advanced in pregnancy, went to Wildbad for further treatment to her leg. Bertie, his old restlessness reasserting itself, rotated between Rompenheim, Homburg and Baden as enthusiastically as ever. In London he now had his own private club—aptly named the Marlborough, situated conveniently in Pall Mall, just across from Marlborough House. He had resigned from White's in a huff when the committee turned down his proposal that smoking should be permitted in the morning room. Piqued at not getting his own way, he decided to have his own club where he could make his own rules and pick his own members. Wealthy friends, eager to ingratiate themselves with the Prince of Wales, were quick to put up the necessary money.

The child conceived in Egypt was born on 26th November 1869. They named her Maud. With Maud in her arms, Bertie at her side, the other children around her, Alix felt, for the moment, happy and fulfilled. The gossip about Harriet Mordaunt, which had first come to her ears months ago, when she and Bertie were still on their travels, seemed trivial and unimportant— just gossip . . .

THE MORDAUNT AFFAIR

Bertie and Alix had been still on their travels that February of 1869 when Harriet Mordaunt, the young wife of Sir Charles Mordaunt, Member of Parliament for Warwickshire, was confined at Walton Hall. The baby was a girl, small and premature, weighing scarcely three and a half pounds. The midwife, Elizabeth Hancock, looking at the finger and toe nails, judged it to be about an eight-month baby. For names, Sir Charles suggested Violet and his wife added Caroline. "After your mother," she said.

Then, suddenly, almost out of the blue, she blurted out something else.

"Charley," she said, "I have deceived you. You are not the father of my child."

Sir Charles was taken aback, scarcely knowing what to think. He told himself that it wasn't true, that Harriet was unwell and disturbed after the ordeal of childbirth. In a few days she would be better and all this nonsense would be forgotten.

It wasn't. Eight days after the baby's birth Harriet Mordaunt again told her husband, "Charley, you are not the father of the child." She burst out sobbing. "Lord Cole is the father."

Her husband looked at her without reply.

"Charley, I have been very wicked," she sobbed. "I have done very wrong."

"With whom?" he asked.

"Lord Cole, Sir Frederick Johnstone and the Prince of Wales and others."

In his wife's escritoire Sir Charles found some hotel bills and some letters signed "Albert Edward". In her diary was an entry for 3rd April still some weeks ahead. It read simply: "280 days from 27th June."

To him, it suggested that 3rd April was the date on which she had expected the baby to be born; 27th June the day on which she had conceived. And on 27th June of the previous year he had been away in Norway, fishing.

There was no longer any doubt in his mind. He told his wife she had dishonoured him, packed his bags, left and instituted divorce proceedings.

As gossip spread, Bertie became an increasingly uneasy young man, worried that a subpoena might be served on him. He was in a cleft stick, as he told his mother in a letter. If he gave evidence in court, there might be an attempt to "turn and twist everything that I say in an attempt to compromise me". If he refused to appear on the other hand, "the public may suppose that I shrink from answering these imputations which have been cast upon me".

Of these alternatives, Alix knew which she preferred. Bertie should appear in court to give lie to the rumours. Queen Victoria agreed. So did the Lord Chancellor, when the Queen consulted him.

In fact, the expected subpoena was never served. Nevertheless, Bertie at his own wish, appeared in court to give evidence.

The case which came before Lord Penzance and a special jury in Westminster Hall in the February of 1870 was not the actual divorce hearing, but a preliminary to it. What the jury had to decide was whether Harriet Mordaunt was in a fit mental state to answer her husband's petition. The court was packed. So many people crowded in on the first day, 16th February, that the gallery, creaking ominously, seemed in danger of collapse. It was later checked for safety and the number of spectators limited.

They listened avidly as Harriet Mordaunt's maid, Jessie Clarke, told of the men in her mistress's life—Captain Farquhar; Lord Cole, who stayed at Walton Hall while Sir Charles was away in Norway; Sir Frederick Johnstone, who called upon her when she was staying in a hotel in London; the Prince of Wales, who often visited her in London, staying an hour, sometimes two hours, alone with her ladyship in the drawing room.

The Mordaunt's butler, Henry Bird, also told of Bertie's visits. He arrived usually in a hansom about four in the afternoon, when Sir Charles was either at the House of Commons or out shooting, and stayed an hour or two.

Sir Charles, in his evidence, said that he knew the Prince of

Wales was an acquaintance of his wife, and he had, he said, warned her "against continuing" the acquaintanceship.

"Why was that?" the Judge wanted to know.

"I had heard in various quarters certain circumstances connected with his previous career which caused me to make the remark," Sir Charles explained.

Daily the evidence was published in *The Times* for Bertie and Alix to read. Whatever she may have thought or felt, Alix was determined not to behave like a deceived wife. So she continued to dine out as usual, to go to the theatre as usual, to drive in the park as usual. One day she even had Bertie take her skating in Regent's Park. Despite her lameness, she could still skate provided she had someone with her with whom to link arms.

Bertie's letters to Harriet Mordaunt were read in court and reprinted in the newspapers. One thanked her for the gift of some "pretty muffetees . . . very useful this cold weather." Another mentioned some ponies he was buying from him. They all began "My dear Lady Mordaunt" and ended "yours most sincerely, Albert Edward".

He would like to see her again, he wrote in one letter. And in another:

"I am so sorry to find by the letter that I received from you this morning that you are unwell, and that I shall not be able to pay you a visit today, to which I had been looking forward with so much pleasure . . . but if you are still in town, may I come to see you about five on Sunday afternoon?"

"Perhaps the most innocent letters that ever a gentleman wrote to a lady," Harriet Mordaunt's counsel commented in court.

On 23rd February, came the moment for which everyone in the crowded, stuffy court room had been waiting.

"His Royal Highness the Prince of Wales," called the usher.

There was a stir and a craning of necks as Bertie entered from an ante-room at the rear of the court, a stoutish, bearded, balding figure.

He took his place at the wooden rail which served as a witness box. The usher handed him a Bible and he took the oath.

"Before your Royal Highness is asked any question," Lord Penzance told him, "I think it is my duty to point out . . . that no witness in these proceedings shall be liable to be asked or bound to answer any question tending to show that he or she has been guilty of adultery."

Bertie bowed stiffly in acknowledgement.

Dr Deane, counsel for Lady Mordaunt, rose and began his questioning in a subdued and deferential voice.

"I believe Your Royal Highness has for some years been acquainted with the Moncreiffe family?"

"I have."

"Were you acquainted with Lady Mordaunt before her marriage?"

"I was."

"On marriage, did Your Royal Highness write to her and make her some wedding present?"

"I did."

"Previous to her marriage had she visited Marlborough House when Your Royal Highness and the Princess of Wales were there?"

"She had."

"And has she gone to the theatre with both Your Royal Highnesses?"

"She has."

"We are told that she was married at the end of 1866. In 1867 did you see much of her?"

"I did."

"We have heard in the course of the case that Your Royal Highness uses hansom cabs occasionally. I do not know whether it is so."

"It is so," Bertie confirmed.

And so, quickly and easily, to the final, all-important question.

"I have only one more question to trouble Your Royal Highness with. Has there ever been any improper familiarity or criminal act between yourself and Lady Mordaunt?"

"Never," said Bertie, emphatically.

Dr Deane sat down again. Despite Bertie's earlier fears, there was no attempt to "turn and twist" what he had said; no cross-examination. In seven minutes it was all over, as far as he was concerned, and a small burst of applause followed him as he left the court.

But it was not until the following day that the evidence on both sides, much of it medical, was finally concluded and the

Alix with her daughters: (left to right) Princesses Maud and Victoria, and Princess Louise (Duchess of Fife)

Eddy (Duke of Clarence) and May (Princess Mary of Teck) on their engagement in 1891

jury retired. They were out only twenty-five minutes. Their verdict was that Lady Mordaunt was in a state of mental disorder which rendered her unfit to contest her husband's petition.

That evening, the case over, Alix went with Bertie to dine with the Gladstones. At a distance, she looked as beautiful and elegant as ever, but, close up, her face showed something of the strain she had been through. For his part, Bertie was no longer worried and uneasy, as he had been prior to his appearance in court. He was now self-satisfied and indignant.

"I trust that the public at large will be satisfied that the gross imputations which have been so wantonly cast upon me are now cleared up," he wrote to his mother.

But not all of the public were as satisfied as he would have wished. There were many who were inclined to think, as *Reynolds News* did, that if it was all so innocent, why should a young married man visit a young married woman at all when her husband was not there? In their eyes, despite all that had been said in court, Bertie was a philandering husband and Alix the wronged wife. She was cheered and clapped when she appeared in public, but hurrahs and handclaps turned to boos and hisses when Bertie was seen.

"The Prince of Wales has learnt by painful experience how carefully he must walk," *The Times* lectured him.

It was to be a short-lived lesson. By November of the same year Queen Victoria was writing to Vicky: "Unfortunately poor Bertie gives much cause for remarks of no good-natured kind. Instead of being more careful since that dreadful business, he is more and more careless. No one looks up to him, though all like him."

Vicky wrote back agreeing: "Bertie is so incautious and so much talked about... The stays at Petersburg, Paris and Wiesbaden and the stories of last January did the mischief."

Earlier, in the immediate aftermath of the Mordaunt affair, the Queen blamed Alix almost as much as she did Bertie. "They lead far too frivolous a life," she wrote at the time, "and are far too intimate with ... a small set of not the best or wisest people who consider being fast the right thing."

Alix, as the Queen knew, was more deeply hurt by the whole business than she either showed or cared to admit. "She has felt everything that passed lately, deeply," the Queen informed

Vicky, "but she is, I think, quite easy as to Bertie's conduct, only regretting him being foolish and imprudent."

Loving Bertie as she did, Alix could tolerate private hurts. But public scandal she could not endure, and the Mordaunt affair was public in the extreme. For weeks after the case was over and done with, it continued to be the subject for public gossip, sniggers and jeers. Satirical pamphlets dealing with Bertie's private life were passed from hand to hand. It was all too much for Alix. Leaving Bertie, trying to get away from it all, she sought refuge at Kimbolton Castle, the country home of her close friend, Lottie, Duchess of Manchester. It was perhaps not the wisest choice and one of which Queen Victoria certainly did not approve.

The Queen continued to remonstrate with her son over his conduct and way of life, showering him with letters of good advice. With the approach of another Ascot, she wrote to him from Balmoral urging him to confine his visits to the races to a maximum of two days and to gather around him only "the really good, steady and distinguished people".

Bertie, despite the Mordaunt case, was hurt and indignant at his mother's letter. "I am over twenty-eight," he wrote back, "and have some considerable knowledge of the world and society." She must permit him to use his own discretion, he informed her. And "whatever ill-natured stories you may hear about me", he asked her never to withdraw her confidence in him until the facts were proved.

He went to Ascot as usual that year and was booed by the public for his pains. But—such is the fickleness of public opinion—the boos changed to cheers when a horse in which he had a part-share romped home a winner.

"You seem in a better temper now, damn you", Bertie quipped at those nearest to him.

Gladstone urged that Bertie should be given a worthwhile job of work which might encourage him to lead "a more manly mode of life". Could he not serve as the Queen's representative in Ireland? Bertie's mother thought not.

That summer, taking the three elder children with her, Alix left England for Denmark, declining to commit herself as to how long she would be away or when she would return. However, the outbreak of the Franco-Prussian war provided Bertie with an excuse to fetch her back. He feared for her safety, he said. There was a warm reunion between the philandering husband and the ever-loving, ever-forgiving wife. Reconciliation had its inevitable consequences and when they went to Sandringham that autumn Alix was again pregnant.

Their carriage took them from Wolferton station to the new bay-windowed residence, red brick with stone dressing, which had replaced the original white-fronted Sandringham. Descending from the carriage, they stood together to read the inscription over the front porch: "This house was built by Albert Edward and Alexandra his wife in the year of our Lord 1870."

Alix hurried upstairs to see if her cluttered sitting room had remained intact, as she had said it must. If the architect had found this impossible, he had at least managed to reproduce it in faithful detail. Quickly Alix cluttered it afresh, as she cluttered every home of the house, with pictures and ornaments, screens and footstools, clocks and candlesticks, books and bric-à-brac. In almost every room there was a profusion of potted plants. In the drawing room, with its painted ceiling and mirrored walls, its windows looking out towards the lake and waterfall, Alix designed an indoor rockery with a statuette of Venus rising from a mass of ferns and roses. Bertie's private sitting room was equally cluttered with photographs, hunting trophies and souvenirs of his travels.

Guests visiting the new Sandringham for the first time found themselves bustled round on tours of inspection which took in the new billiards room with its concealed wash-basin, the new bowling alley with its smoking room modelled on one Bertie had seen in Turkey, its gun room and vast game room, its wine cellars, kennels and stables.

On 9th November, Bertie's twenty-ninth birthday, he and Alix gave a combined birthday and house-warming party. Bertie, in knickerbockers and a belted Norfolk jacket, a soft felt hat on his head, took the men of the house-party shooting in Woodcock Woods. Like all Bertie's shoots, it was an affair of pomp and pageantry conducted with all the thoroughness of a military operation. It started with a parade of the gamekeepers in their billycock hats and green velveteen suits and the beaters in their country smocks and scarlet-banded hats. The guests, each with two guns and two loaders, drove out in a convoy of

horse-drawn wagonettes, while Bertie, an Inverness cape draped
about his shoulders, supervised things from his pony. When
everyone was in position, the head gamekeeper, also mounted,
sounded a call on his hunting horn as a signal for the beaters to
start putting up the birds with a flurry of flags and a great
banging of improvised tin drums.

Sometimes as many as two thousand birds would be slaugh-
tered in a single day, with cigars and brandy to while away the
time between drives. As a shot, Bertie was variable; never in the
top rank. But he was keen. To allow himself more hours of
daylight in the shooting field he introduced what his friends
referred to as "Sandringham time", setting the clocks there
half-an-hour ahead of the rest of the country. Even the clock on
the parish church was put forward. Alix was less enthused by all
this shooting. She might join Bertie and his guests in the shooting field for a picnic lunch, but she could barely suppress a
shudder at the sight of the bloodstained heaps of dead birds.

To mark his birthday, Bertie arranged a feast of beef, plum
pudding and beer in the coach-house for the estate workers. For
his houseguests there was a dinner party at night, with additional
guests from the county invited for the ball which followed. The
soft glow of the new gas lighting illuminated the front of the
house as they drove up in their carriages. In the oak-panelled
Saloon, with its beamed ceiling and twin fireplaces, the family
portrait above one reflected in the gilt mirror above the other,
the carpet had been removed and the faces of musicians peered
down between the antlers adorning the gallery. The dancing
opened with a quadrille and went on until four in the morning.

Proud and happy in their new home, Bertie and Alix turned
their life at Sandringham into one long house party. Each
Monday morning the "Prince of Wales special" would steam in
from London with a batch of guests who were met at the station
by a cavalcade of carriages, horse buses and luggage brakes. They
stayed until Thursday evening—and on Friday a fresh batch
would arrive to replace them.

Guests breakfasted at nine o'clock and the day's shooting began
promptly at quarter past ten (Sandringham time). Lunch would
be served in a marquee near the shooting area. If the weather was
too bad for shooting, guests were left to their own devices until
midday when Bertie and Alix joined them for lunch. There was

always plenty to do—gossip to be whispered, letters written. Female guests devoted much of their time to changing their clothes: morning dresses for breakfast, tweeds for lunch, tea gowns for the afternoons and evening gowns for dinner at night. The children usually joined the adults for afternoon tea and Queen Victoria was not alone in thinking her grandchildren badly brought up. Some of the guests thought the same, though neither Alix nor Bertie seemed to notice that their children ran almost wild.

Dinner was served at nine o'clock in the oak-panelled dining room with its Goya tapestries and its dominating portrait of Bertie in the uniform of the 10th Hussars. He took a different woman, invariably an attractive one, in to dinner each night. Up to thirty people would sit down round the vast, candle-lit table, the ladies in their long gowns, the men wearing decorations, with Bertie and Alix facing each other across the middle of the table. Conversation was always animated, sometimes noisy. After dinner there would be billiards or bowls, whist or poker, baccarat played for small stakes. Sometimes Alix would join one of the guests for a duet on the grand piano in the Saloon. Sometimes there would be dancing to the music of a barrel-organ, with Bertie taking his turn at cranking the handle. No lady could retire for the night until Alix did and no man until Bertie had had enough—and he stayed up always until the small hours.

On Christmas Eve, an almost excessively jovial Bertie and an Alix who was elegant still in pregnancy stood together in the stable yard, distributing joints of beef to gamekeepers and foresters, stable hands and gardeners. Later, in the Saloon, where a lofty Christmas tree brushed the ceiling, they distributed other gifts—china and cutlery, perfume and cut-throat razors—to servants and secretaries, equerries and ladies-in-waiting.

It was another hard, cold winter, with skating on the lake and impromptu games of ice hockey in which Bertie joined with enthusiasm. Alix skated very little, though not because of her lame leg. She abstained because of pregnancy.

BIRTH AND DEATH

The baby was born on 6th April 1871. It was another premature
birth. Bertie and Alix were again at Sandringham and, as at
Frogmore when Eddy was born, nothing was ready: no baby
clothes, no physician or nurse in attendance. As soon as it became
clear that Alix was in labour, a servant was hurriedly despatched
in search of the nearest doctor.

The baby was a tiny thing, so small and weak that others who
saw it despaired of its life right from the start. Alix, too, looking
at the little mite, knew that the odds were against it. Yet she
continued to hope.

They decided to christen the child that same evening, just in
case. The christening service was kept as short and simple as
possible. They named the baby Alexander John Charles Albert.

When Bertie came to see her the following morning Alix
knew that her hopes had not been fulfilled. His face was drained
of colour and his eyes misted with tears.

He sat on the bed, took her in his arms and they cried on each
other's shoulders.

Estate carpenters hammered together a tiny coffin and Bertie
himself lifted the tiny body into it. Then, with Eddy on one side
and Georgie on the other, he followed the coffin across the park
to a funeral service in the parish church. A stricken Alix watched
the small, sad procession from an upstairs window. In the years
to come she was often to visit the tiny grave, in the shadow of
the churchyard wall, where her last child lay buried.

Queen Victoria, when she heard what had happened, blamed
Bertie. His way of life had encouraged Alix to neglect her health,
she said.

Bertie, resilient as ever, recovered from the shock of this small,
personal tragedy much more quickly than Alix did and within
days he was going around saying that he would be glad when
Alix felt up to resuming her "social duties". Alix had little desire
to do anything of the sort. Even before the birth and death of the
baby, something in her had changed. She was no longer the gay,
fun-loving Alix of early marriage. These days she infinitely
preferred the quiet and seclusion of Sandringham to the social
whirl of Marlborough House.

But that strong sense of duty which Vicky had noted in her years ago drove her, in time, to resume her "social duties". And that summer, while Bertie was in France, she took the children to Rumpenheim for the customary family gathering. Her mother was there; Minnie and Sasha; her other sister, Thyra; and the Cambridge family. The formerly flirtatious Mary Adelaide, blonde and buxom, was now married to Prince Francis of Teck and had with her her four-year-old daughter, Victoria Mary— May for short. Bertie, too, joined the party in due course, but was quickly bored by the endless family chit-chat and moved on to Homburg, where there was more fun to be had.

Back home again, he and Alix were invited to a house party at Lady Londesborough's house near Scarborough. Bertie enjoyed the shooting, and the food and entertainment were excellent. But the drains were no better than those at Windsor and by the time they went to Sandringham on 21st November, Bertie was suffering from a slight fever. So was his groom, Charles Blegge.

TYPHOID

Bertie lay in his blue and white bedroom at Sandringham, tossing and turning, feverish and delirious. Alix, her face strained, sat at the bedside, ministering to him. At times he was so delirious he did not recognize her.

"You're a good boy," he told her, perhaps mistaking her for Eddy or Georgie.

"I am Alix your wife," she told him, quietly.

"That was once but is no more," he mumbled, deliriously. "You have broken your vows."

His mind rambling more and more, he was full of feverish remorse, begging her forgiveness for past wickedness. For once perhaps, Alix was fortunate in her deafness. It prevented her from hearing some of the things he said in his delirium. But she could lip-read others and on one occasion, her face white and shocked, had to be hurried from the sick room because of what her husband revealed in his ravings.

Dr Gull, hastily summoned to Sandringham, had diagnosed mild typhoid fever. The children were packed off to stay with Queen Victoria, who straightaway sent Sir William Jenner to reinforce Gull. Alix moved out of her own bedroom, and into Bertie's dressing room. Along with her sister-in-law, Alice, who was staying at Sandringham at the time, Lady Macclesfield, and Bertie's valet, she took her turn at nursing Bertie.

Frantic with worry though she was, she also found time to go across the yard to inquire how Blegge, the groom, was in his room above the stable. She went every day while the illness of the two men, groom and prince, ran its course.

Bertie's condition became rapidly worse. By the end of a week it was so critical that Queen Victoria was summoned. Accompanied by John Brown, her now indispensable servant, she arrived at Wolferton by special train on 29th November. Affie met her at the station and they drove to Sandringham through plantations of young, new fir trees. It was the first time the Queen had visited Sandringham and she remarked that the landscape was flat and bleak.

Alix and Alice were waiting for her at the front door. Alix, anxious looking, with tears in her eyes, was thinner even than usual, the Queen thought. They took her upstairs to Bertie's room. He was asleep, his breathing rapid and stertorous. His pulse and temperature were both up, the doctors whispered. Only a single lamp burnt in the otherwise darkened room as the Queen peered at him from around the screen which had been erected to ward off draughts. Then, quietly, she crept out again and joined Alix in her cluttered sitting room. Alix was almost beside herself with worry, reminding her mother-in-law vividly of those terrible days at Windsor which had preceded the death of Bertie's father.

Almost as though his mother's royal visit had worked something in the nature of a miracle, Bertie weathered the immediate crisis and showed signs of improvement. By 1st December he was sufficiently improved for the Queen to return to Windsor.

"What date is it?" he wanted to know.

Told it was 1st December, he looked pleased. "The Princess's birthday," he commented. Alix was twenty-seven.

But the same day also brought news of the death of Lord Chesterfield. He, like Bertie, had been at Londesborough Lodge for the shooting.

On 7th December Bertie had a relapse. A restless night of rapid respiration, with his temperature up to 104, was followed by another day of high fever and delirium. He whistled, sang and laughed to himself as he tossed in his sweaty bed, raving of all the things he would do as soon as he was King, talking of other things better left unsaid.

Jenner and Gull despaired of his life. "If he does not rally within the hour," one of them confided in the other, "a few more hours must see the end."

Queen Victoria was warned that "there seems hardly any hope left". Once again she set off for Sandringham. Alice and her husband, Louis of Hesse, were already there. Affie had left, but returned that evening, driving through deep snow. Louise, Leopold and Beatrice turned up too. It was difficult to find house room for so many and Louise and Beatrice began to bicker when they found they had to share the same bedroom, while the Queen was irritated at finding the clocks half-an-hour fast. It was all too much for Alix, already unnerved by worry and anxiety. She fled to her bedroom and prayed at her bedside. Later, trudging across the park through snow that was fast turning to slush, she prayed again in the parish church.

10th December was a Sunday. Alix attended evensong in the parish church, seeking out the parson and asked him to pray for "my darling husband" early in the service so that she could join in. She could not stay long, she explained, as she must get back to his bedside.

She stayed with Bertie all that night and was still there at half-past five in the morning when the Queen, in her dressing gown, crept into the candle-lit bedroom to join her. Bertie, breathing heavily, talking incessantly, seemed totally unaware of their presence. They must expect the end at any time, the doctors warned them.

By seven o'clock the whole family was congregated round the door of the sickroom, their faces strained and bewildered, their eyes moist. "The awfulness of this morning I shall never forget as long as I live," the Duke of Cambridge noted in his diary.

But two days later Bertie was still alive. Weak, breathing feebly, talking incoherently, his talk broken by fits of coughing . . . but still fighting for life. Alix was close to breakdown. The Queen put her arm comfortingly around her and told her there was still hope. But to Alice she confided differently: "There can be no hope," she said.

Even more than Alix she dreaded the dawn of 14th December—the tenth anniversary of the death of Bertie's father. Was Bertie, too, to be taken on that ill-fated day?

But that night Bertie's fever abated slightly and he was no longer delirious. His mother went over to the bed, took his thin, hot hand in hers and kissed it.

He looked at her vacantly. "Who are you?" he asked. Recognition dawned in his bulging eyes. "Mama," he said.

"Dear child," murmured the Queen.

"It's so kind of you to come," Bertie mumbled.

The Queen sat down at the bedside. Bertie looked surprised. "Don't sit here for me," he said. But, later, he was again feverish, his breathing again quick and his hands clutching at objects that weren't there.

That night of 14th December—the anniversary of his father's death—he had a few hours of sound, untroubled sleep. Next day he again recognized his mother, but had no recollection of seeing her before.

"Dear Mama," he said, "I am so glad to see you. Have you been here all this time?"

Day by day, little by little, Bertie improved, and Alix was beside herself with joy. But in his room above the stables, where she still called each day, Blegge, the groom, was getting worse instead of better, ever more feverish and delirious. On 17th December he died. Alix went to his funeral and, later, she and Bertie paid for a tombstone to be erected over his grave.

By 19th December, Bertie seemed well enough for the Queen to return to Windsor. By the New Year, though there had been another brief relapse meantime, he was on the road to full recovery. Sandringham was quiet again now, the visitors all gone.

To Alix, what had happened seemed like some awful nightmare through which she had been forced to live and somehow managed to survive. But, looking at Bertie, no longer as fat as he had been, she felt that his recovery was reward enough for all her worry and fears. Now, in convalescence, she had him all to herself. It was like being on a second honeymoon, she confided in the motherly Lady Macclesfield. God, she felt, had listened to her prayers and given her back her life's happiness.

To the little church in which she had prayed Alix donated a

brass lectern inscribed "to The Glory Of God—a thanksgiving for His Mercy" together with the date—14th December 1871—on which she felt her husband had turned the corner.

Bertie, too, was grateful for his recovery, full of remorse for things past, full of high hopes for the future. What he wanted more than anything now, he said, was to lead a life of usefulness to the country. For Alix he had nothing but praise and affection.

"What her devotion, tenderness and affection were to me during my long illness can never be known," he wrote. "She was like an angel of light hovering over me and dispelling the dark angel of death."

To Alix, the ordeal through which she had passed as Bertie hovered between life and death, was an essentially personal thing. She shared with her mother-in-law—who thought it "too much show"—a degree of distaste for Disraeli's idea of a national thanksgiving service. Left to her own devices, she would have preferred something simpler and quieter. But the people of Britain, she agreed, had shared her anxiety and had a right now to share her joy.

The thanksgiving service was held on 27th February. Bertie, convalescent and still weak, one leg still swollen, limped to the state landau which was to take them to St Paul's. Alix was in blue velvet and sable; Queen Victoria in the inevitable black, trimmed with miniver. The streets were decked with flags and lined with troops. Military bands played and there was a Sovereign's escort of cavalry. Moved by the emotion of the moment, the Queen, as the procession reached Temple Bar, raised her son's hand to her lips and kissed it. The crowds cheered deafeningly, the kissing and boo-ing of a year ago completely forgotten. Tears glistened in Bertie's protuberant blue eyes.

SEPARATE WAYS

The remorse and penitence Bertie felt in the immediate aftermath of illness, his resolve to be a better man in the future, was sadly short-lived.

In March 1871, with Alix, he set off on a three-month convalescent cruise. They went first to Paris; then on to Cannes where the royal yacht awaited them. At Rome they met up with

Alix's parents. Thyra and Waldemar, her younger sister and brother, were with them. Together, they visited Florence, Venice, Como. It was the start of a pattern of life which was to continue for years to come.

In March each year they would leave Sandringham for Cannes or some other Mediterranean sunspot, stopping off in Paris en route. For Bertie, there were also other—bachelor—excursions to the French capital. And a new attraction there—Sarah Bernhardt with her sapphire-green eyes, red-blonde hair and seductively gliding walk. Visiting Paris, Bertie was often to be found in her dressing room at the theatre or at her house on the corner of the Rue Fortuny. When she played in Sardou's *Fedora*, he thought it a great lark to appear briefly on stage with her in the role of her murdered lover.

The start of the London season would find Bertie and Alix back at Marlborough House for a social programme which included a garden party, two balls and innumerable dinner parties. With the public, Alix was more popular than ever and crowds lined the streets around Marlborough House to see her drive out in her barouche. With Bertie, she went to Ascot, Goodwood, Cowes. She did not share his enthusiasm for racing, but enjoying the sailing.

With the end of the London season, they went their separate ways, Alix for a cruise with the children, to Denmark to see her parents or to Bayreuth for the music, Bertie to Baden or Homburg for the races, the gambling, the women.

September found them together again at Abergeldie, where Bertie went stag shooting. Then it was south to Sandringham for the pheasant and partridge shooting and a succession of house parties. There were other house parties elsewhere to which Bertie sometimes went without Alix.

There was never any lack of people eager to entertain the Prince of Wales, costly though the operation was. It meant accommodating not only Bertie himself, but the latest of his feminine 'pets', his friends of the so-called 'Marlborough House set', two equerries and at least seven servants. It meant redecorating, sometimes redesigning, the suite of rooms he would occupy. It meant arranging diversions—hunting, shooting, baccarat, a ball—to keep him from being bored. It all cost a great deal of money and some, like Christopher Sykes, went bankrupt in the process.

Bertie soon regained the weight lost through illness. He was an enormous eater and a heavy smoker who thought nothing of smoking his way through twenty cigarettes and over a dozen huge cigars in a day. He ate five big meals—breakfast, lunch, afternoon tea, dinner and supper—a day. He would eat his way through bacon, eggs, haddock, woodcock. And that was just breakfast. Dinner ran to ten or more courses, each richer and more exotic than the one before—caviar, turtle soup, oysters (which he loved), eggs in aspic, pigeon pie, snipe stuffed with foie gras, woodcock stuffed with truffles, ortolans done in brandy. And even five meals was sometimes not enough. Mid-morning and the early hours of the following morning would find him tucking into a snack to keep him going.

Alix, by contrast, ate sparingly, avoiding the rich, exotic dishes on which Bertie doted. She ate plenty of fruit and vegetables; drank lots of milk. This combination of small meals and the right food did wonders for her figure and complexion. While Bertie grew ever plumper, she remained slim and young-looking.

Just as there were always wealthy friends eager to host the Prince of Wales, so there was never any lack of attractive women ready to jump into bed with him. In 1873 Bertie's private secretary, Francis Knollys, was hunting round for a discreet London *pied-à-terre* where Bertie and Affie, his younger, heavy-drinking brother, might meet their lady friends. In 1874 Bertie spent a hectic two weeks in France which included a visit to the Chateau de Mello, home of the beautiful, extravagant Princess de Sagan. In 1875 there was another visit to Mello, when the son of the house, finding Bertie's trousers in his mother's boudoir, tossed them out of the window into the fountain in the courtyard.

Alix continued to turn a blind eye to Bertie's infidelities. Now so deaf that she found conversation difficult and was increasingly stiff in her manner on that account, she sought consolation in her children, her few friends, her family. In 1873 she had Minnie over from Russia to stay with her. To the delight of those who saw them, the two sisters often appeared in public dressed exactly alike.

The children were growing up. When Alix and Bertie

journeyed to St Petersburg in January 1874, for Affie's wedding
to the Tsar's daughter, they left Eddy, now ten, and Georgie,
nearing nine, in charge of a tutor, John Dalton. Both boys
adored their mother, but held their father in the same awe that
he had once held his father.

If Alix sometimes grieved over Bertie's way of life, there was
concern too in high places. Gladstone felt that a worthwhile job
of work might convert him to a better way of life. But Queen
Victoria had no desire still to surrender even a fraction of her
regal power. And Bertie, for all his assurance that he wished to
live "a life of usefulness to the country", seemed hardly more
enthused.

Some minor royal chores came his way. With Alix, he toured
Coventry and Birmingham. Lord Hartington and his mistress,
Lottie, were also in the party. Bertie was largely bored. At
Coventry, to enliven the proceedings, he asked for a bowling
alley to be included in the tour itinerary for Hartington's benefit.
"Inform the mayor", he chortled, "that his lordship is a great
games player and particularly fond of skittles." Skittles, of
course, was Catherine Walters.

More to Bertie's liking was the fancy dress ball for 1400 guests
he gave at Marlborough House in July 1874. It was, everyone
agreed, the most ostentatiously extravagant entertainment ever
held there. All Bertie's friends were there, Harty-Tarty dressed as
a Venetian grandee, Lottie also in Venetian costume, the
Beresford brothers—Marcus and Charles—as jesters in cap and
bells. Bertie, a mass of cavalier curls concealing his baldness, was
Charles I in a suit of maroon satin and velvet. Alix, in a jewelled
cap and a gown of ruby velvet embroidered in silver and gold,
was a Venetian princess.

While Alix, in a strange way, understood and overlooked
Bertie's infidelities, there were other things she found it less easy
to forgive. One of these was when she found he was planning a
tour of India which did not include her. Hurt, disappointed,
indignant, she demanded to know why she could not go with
him. He made all manner of excuses, but the truth was that he
did not want her.

She went over his head and appealed to Disraeli, Gladstone,
Queen Victoria herself. They agreed with Bertie. She had five
children to look after, she was reminded.

"The husband has first claim," she retorted.

His departure left her very depressed. To cheer herself up, she invited her parents and Thyra over from Denmark. When they returned, she went with them, taking the children. She made no attempt to obtain her mother-in-law's approval first and the Queen was furious.

Bertie, meantime, was thoroughly enjoying himself, travelling in style with a party of over forty . . . servants, equerries, friends of the Marlborough House set, among them Lord Aylesford.

20th February 1876, found them in camp along the Sardah River. There was nothing rough and ready about the royal camp; every conceivable Victorian luxury was laid on. That night, while Bertie was changing for dinner, Aylesford came to see him, flourishing a letter he had received from his attractive, Welsh-born wife. She was in love with Lord Blandford (a married man), she wrote, and they were going off together.

Bertie was almost as indignant as Aylesford himself. Blandford was the biggest blackguard alive, he said. Aylesford must leave at once and institute divorce proceedings.

Among the Marlborough House set, divorce meant social ostracism and the mere thought of this was sufficient to frighten Aylesford's wife. She promptly disentangled herself from Blandford and begged her husband not to proceed with the divorce. He refused.

Alix, returning home from Denmark, soon heard the gossip that was going round about Lady Aylesford and Lord Blandford. Even so, it came as a surprise when Blandford's younger brother, Lord Randolph Churchill, walrus-moustached and sharp-tongued, called at Marlborough House to see her.

She must use her influence to get Aylesford to withdraw his divorce petition, Churchill told her. If she did not—if the case came to court—the Prince of Wales would be subpoenaed and letters he had written to Lady Aylesford would be read in evidence. And if that happened, Churchill added, Bertie could never expect to sit upon the throne of England.

In Bertie's absence, poor Alix scarcely knew what to do. There was only one other person to whom to turn. She ordered her carriage round and set off to see her mother-in-law.

Bertie was in Cairo, on his way home, when he learned of Churchill's threats. Furious, he sent his close friend, Charles

Beresford, on ahead of him to challenge Churchill to a duel on his behalf. A duel between the Prince of Wales and Churchill was, of course, "impossible and absurd", but Churchill would have been better not to have said so in a defiant reply which made Bertie even more furious.

Churchill could publish his letters and be hanged to him, he said. He would simply stay out of the country until the whole affair had blown over. His main regret was that Alix had been dragged into things and he wrote her a tender and contrite letter. When he did return, he wrote, he wanted to see her "first and alone".

Queen Victoria, anxious to avoid another royal scandal, called in Disraeli who could bring pressure to bear in the right places. As a result, she was able to write to Bertie in due course that there was little prospect of "a public scandal". He could safely return home.

Aylesford withdrew his divorce petition, though Lady Blandford separated from her husband. Randolph Churchill wrote Bertie a grudging letter of apology before heading for the United States with his American-born wife, Jennie. The grudging apology was grudgingly accepted, but several years were to go by before Bertie forgave Churchill sufficiently to sit at the same table with him again.

On his return home, looking as tanned and fit as he had ever looked in his life, he met Alix "first and alone", as he had suggested in his letter. While the children and others awaited his arrival in Portsmouth, a tender took her out to the converted troopship *Seraphis* while it was still off the Needles.

That night, as after the Mordaunt case, her head held high, she drove with him through London. They were on their way to occupy the royal box at Covent Garden.

Four generations: (*left*) The King and Queen of Denmark, their daughter Alix, granddaughter Louise (Duchess of Fife) and the Lady Alexandra Duff (1892); (*right*) Queen Victoria, Alix, May, and David—the infant Duke of Windsor—at his christening at White Lodge, Richmond, 1894

Four Kings: (*left to right*) George V, Edward VII, Edward VIII and George VI

PART FOUR

The Mistresses

LILLIE LANGTRY

Bertie, normally something of a clockwatcher, was somewhat late for the supper party Sir Allen Young was giving at his home in Stratford Place. He had been to the opera and had come straight on, still wearing his decorations and the blue Garter ribbon. It was 24th May 1877.

"I am afraid I'm a little late," he apologized as he joined his host and eight other guests in the drawing room. His eyes strayed to the clearly uncorseted figure of the blonde with violet eyes and fair, almost transparent skin who was standing by the mantelpiece.

She was presented to him. "Mrs Langtry, Sir." She curtsied.

The other guests were presented in turn, among them Edward Langtry, her plump, Irish-born husband. In them Bertie betrayed only polite, princely interest. It was the fascinating Mrs Langtry he had come to meet. He had heard all about her from Leopold, his younger brother, who had met her at a dinner party given by the Marchioness of Ely. Leopold was so captivated by her that he had bought a drawing the artist Frank Miles had done of her and hung it over his bed.

Bertie took her in to supper that night. Normally gay and vivacious, she was unaccountably nervous for once and said little. Bertie asked if he might call upon her at her home in Norfolk Street, a small red-brick house with smokey chimneys next door to a public house. Smilingly, she acceded. That was the start of it.

When Alix, her health again troubling her, had left for Greece earlier in the year to spend a few weeks with her brother, the King of the Hellenes, hardly anyone outside a small, tight, artistic circle had heard of Lillie Langtry. By the time Alix returned, there was hardly anyone who had not heard of the "Jersey Lily". Her picture was in all the shops along with those of the other so-called 'professional beauties' of the day. Her newfound fame—or notoriety—stemmed from the fact that she was the latest acknowledged 'pet' of the Prince of Wales.

Bertie was now thirty-five; Lillie was twenty-three, the daughter of the Dean of Jersey, the only girl in a family of seven, christened Emilie Charlotte le Breton. She had taught briefly in the local Sunday school before marrying Edward Langtry, a thirty-year-old widower with sufficient income to enable him to idle his time away yachting and fishing.

He brought her to London. There, out walking one day, they ran into Lord Ranelagh who had met Lillie previously in Jersey. Ranelagh introduced them, in turn, to Lady Sebright and Lillie was launched into fashionable society. In the only evening gown she possessed at the time, a simple black creation made by a local dressmaker in Jersey, she took London by storm. Men were fascinated by her and Lillie revelled in it. Sir John Millais wanted to paint her and she sat for him in his studio at Palace Gate. Edward Poynter, George Frederick Watts, James MacNeil Whistler and Sir Edward Burne-Jones all painted her in turn. Millais' portrait of her was exhibited at the Royal Academy. He called it *The Jersey Lily*, which gave her her nickname.

Bertie, from the moment of their first meeting, was captivated by her to an extent where discretion went out of the window. He not only made her his mistress, but proclaimed the fact publicly by driving her around in his carriage and riding with her in Rotten Row.

Alix not only accepted the fact that her husband now had a mistress, but condoned it, as though by doing so she could make the relationship seem other than what it was. She acted as though Lillie was as much her friend as Bertie's. They made a curious trio that season of 1877, the wife, the husband and the mistress, riding together in Rotten Row, strolling together on the trim lawns of the Royal Yacht Squadron at Cowes, taking tea together aboard the royal yacht *Osborne*.

Bertie and Lillie, at this stage of their relationship, were almost inseparable. When Bertie and Alix went to Cowes, Lillie went too—staying with Allen Young aboard his schooner. When Bertie went to stay with Ferdinand de Rothschild at Goodwood, Lillie and her husband were invited too. Alix had her to dinner at Marlborough House; and invited her to Sandringham for Bertie's birthday ball that November.

But if Alix accepted the situation, Edward Langtry did not. There were angry scenes in the plum-coloured drawing room at 17 Norfolk Street.

But rave as her husband might, Lillie was not prepared to relinquish the triumph and adulation she enjoyed as Bertie's mistress. She went everywhere she was invited—to receptions, concerts, dinners, balls, sometimes going on from one ball to another so as to take in four or five in a single night, dancing until dawn, then returning home to change into her riding clothes and canter along Rotten Row on her hack Redskin.

She found, as others did before and after, that keeping up with Bertie cost a great deal of money. A single black evening gown was no longer sufficient. She needed a constant supply of new clothes—for Marlborough House, for Ascot, for Sandown— elaborate, expensive gowns like the one she had made of yellow tulle covered with gold fishnet enclosing a flutter of artificial butterflies. She needed a carriage of her own. The house in Norfolk Street needed more servants—a butler, maids, grooms and a coachman. It all cost money. Despite his protests, her cuckold of a husband paid—and paid—and paid.

Another new gown, low-necked and short-sleeved, was required when, during Lillie's second London season, Bertie arranged for her to be presented at one of the Queen's Drawing Rooms at Buckingham Palace. Just before leaving for the palace she received a huge bouquet of Maréchal Ney roses—a gift from Bertie—exactly matching the embroidered roses on the new gown of ivory brocade. She was both nervous and excited as her brougham joined the long line of carriages, with their bewigged coach-men and powdered footmen, waiting outside the palace. It was a stiflingly hot day. A military band played in the palace forecourt. The Household Cavalry formed a guard of honour. Beefeaters in their quaint Elizabethan costumes were on duty at the doors.

Lillie was the last but two to be presented. Normally, after receiving the long line of debutantes for the first half-hour or so, Queen Victoria would withdraw and let Alix take over. But this day she did not. Perhaps the Queen was curious to see this "Jersey Lily" about whom she had heard so much. Perhaps Alix herself felt that for her to take over was really asking too much. Either way, the Queen stayed on.

"Mrs Langtry comes next, Your Majesty," the Lord Chamberlain announced as Lillie handed her train to the waiting pages.

Clutching Bertie's yellow roses, trembling a little from nerves, her face veiled with white tulle, three long ostrich plumes in her hair, Lillie approached and curtsied while the pages behind her spread her train in the approved fashion.

Queen Victoria, in her customary black with a velvet train, the blue ribbon of the Garter across her bodice, continued to gaze straight ahead of her. She looked, Lillie thought, a little tired. The Queen extended a podgy hand. Lillie kissed it.

That evening Lillie was one of the guests—Vicky and Fritz were there, too—at Marlborough House. Bertie was in high spirits and teased her about the length of the ostrich plumes she had worn at his mother's Drawing Room.

Unfaithful husband though he was, Bertie was a good father. His sons, he was resolved, should have a different, better upbringing than he had had, with more company of boys of their own age. With this in mind, he suggested that they should become naval cadets aboard the old wooden training ship *Britannia* at Dartmouth. His mother, when she heard, did not agree at all. She wanted her grandsons to go to Wellington College, but Dalton, their tutor, felt that they were not up to the required educational standard. Alix, doting on the boys, inclined to baby them still for all that they were now in their early teens, did not really want them to go away at all. Eddy, she was sure, weakly and sensitive as he was, would never settle down to the rough, physical life aboard a cadet training ship.

Alix's fears concerning Eddy were to prove well-founded. When the time came to join *Britannia* he was ill in bed and both boys were kept back until he had recovered. Eddy was tall for his age; Georgie on the small side. But brighter and more robust than his elder brother, he did well from the start, revelling in this new, spartan way of life which started with a cold tub at half-past six in the morning. Eddy, by contrast, proved so backward that his parents were urged to take him away again. Bertie would not hear of it and Alix agreed that the boys should not be separated. By keeping them together, both parents hoped, some of Georgie's brightness might rub off on Eddy.

Alix's parents and her sister, Thyra, again came to stay at

Marlborough House that year of 1878. Thyra was downcast and depressed over an unfortunate love affair. For six years, since she had first met him in Rome as a girl of nineteen, she had nurtured a secret passion for Prince Ernst Augustus of Hanover. But political considerations of first one sort, then another, had intervened between them and marriage. She was now twenty-six and marriage seemed as far away as ever.

Alix recalled her own secret meeting with Bertie in the cathedral at Speyer, years before. Why could Thyra and Ernst not meet in the same secret fashion and see if things could not now be resolved? So she wrote to Ernst's sisters suggesting a meeting in Frankfurt when the family were next at Rumpenheim. The meeting duly took place and, to Thyra's joy and Alix's delight, her matchmaking efforts were crowned with success.

Alix's thirty-fourth birthday in December, found them at Sandringham as usual. "My Bertie quite overloaded me with lovely presents," she wrote to his mother in the same letter in which she thanked the Queen for a brooch and, still more, for "your affectionate letter".

"From the first day of my landing in England", Alix wrote to her mother-in-law, "you have always shown me such invariable kindness that I should indeed be ungrateful if I did not do my best in every way to show how much I appreciated it. Thanks, a thousand thanks, for all your loving kindness."

From Sandringham, she and Bertie travelled to Windsor, as every year, for the annual memorial service to Bertie's dead father. They arrived there on the evening of 13th December to be greeted with the news that Bertie's sister, Alice, ill with diphtheria at Darmstadt, was in an "altogether more favourable state".

The relief they and Queen Victoria felt at this welcome news was short-lived. Other telegrams arrived during the night giving different and conflicting news of Alice's condition and by morning all three were in a state of superstitious apprehension. This was the date on which Bertie's father had died; the date on which Bertie himself had so very nearly died. Would Alice—the girl to whom Wally Paget had once likened Alix—survive or be taken?

The look on the Queen's face told Alix and Bertie the sad

news even before she showed them the latest telegram clutched in her shaking hand. It was from Alice's husband: "Poor Mama, poor me, my happiness gone, dear, dear Alice."

"It is the good who are always taken," murmured Bertie. To him, Alice was "my favourite sister . . . so good, so kind, so clever".

But it was Alix who comforted the Queen most in this hour of fresh grief. "Dear Alix has been a real devoted sympathizing daughter," the Queen noted.

Still infatuated with Lillie Langtry, Bertie continued to live at as fast a pace as ever, still spent money as though it grew on trees. At Sandringham he had a new waterworks constructed and a new lake with an island in the middle. Soon he was planning a new ballroom, with new stables to follow as racing became his latest enthusiasm.

Eddy and Georgie finished their spell aboard *Britannia*. Georgie had done well. Eddy had proved a conspicuous failure, so dull that some of his instructors thought him "backward". Alix still doted on him, but Bertie had little more time for a backward son than he had for a deaf wife. A spell at sea, he thought, might help to make a man of him and he arranged for both boys to join H.M.S. *Bacchante* for a seven-month cruise to the West Indies. A spell at home would be followed by a longer cruise to Australia, China and Japan.

Georgie was thoroughly excited at the prospect; Eddy was unenthused and Alix upset. Eddy was now sixteen, 5 feet 5 inches tall, but she still thought of them both as small children. "Poor little boys," she called them in a letter to Queen Victoria.

The Queen, at first, was not in favour of her grandsons going to sea. Then she changed her ideas. At least, it would get the boys away from the sort of people with whom Alix and Bertie were so fond of mixing. This was something that constantly troubled her. She spoke to Bertie about it; wrote to Alix about it. The "dear boys" must be kept away from the society of "fashionable and fast people".

Irritated, Bertie assured his mother that her grandsons did not mix with "fashionable society". And even if they did, he added contradictorily, they were "so simple and innocent that those they have come in contact with have such tact with them that they are not likely to do them any harm".

Plumper than ever from years of good living, Bertie was sometimes boyish still, sometimes pompous. More and more he resented criticism and would sometimes still fly into one of those rages which had been common in childhood. But an attractive woman could twist him round her little finger. He was delighted when La Goulue, the lead dancer at the Moulin Rouge, greeted him disrespectfully, "Ullo, Wales". But a male friend who addressed him in much the same fashion during a game of billiards quickly found himself on his way home in his carriage.

Bertie and Alix went to Spithead to see the boys off on their trip to the West Indies. The parting upset Alix so much that Bertie, leaving Lillie to her own devices for a time, took her to Denmark to visit her parents.

With the boys gone, Alix felt more lonely and deserted than ever. All the time they were away she wrote them gushing and affectionate letters and was never happier than when her mail included a return letter to "Motherdear", as all her children called her. Now she had only the girls—Louise, Victoria and Maud—for company and she kept them close to her. More and more, her children, her home, her religion and her charities served as some sort of compensation for Bertie's unfaithfulness.

At Sandringham she became an increasingly familiar sight as she jogged round in her pony trap, visiting the aged and infirm, sometimes calling at isolated cottages as late as ten or eleven o'clock at night with medicine for someone who was sick or hot soup for the old. At one cottage she sat down by the fire and finished some socks the occupant was knitting. Another time, coming across an old woman trudging alone heavily laden, she stopped to find out who she was and later bought her a donkey.

As news of her generosity spread around begging letters arrived by the sackload. Diligently Alix ploughed through them, picking out those she thought genuine and deserving, sending money or arranging for the letter-writers to be helped in other ways.

The London Hospital was her favourite charity. She became president of the committee and took the job so seriously that she would descend unexpectedly on hospital and staff, wandering through the wards, sitting beside beds, chatting to nurses and patients alike.

She still treated Lillie Langtry as a friend—and not only for the benefit of the public. In a curious way, Alix really liked Lillie and she was both sympathetic and concerned when Lillie was suddenly taken unwell while dining at Marlborough House one evening in 1880. Alix ordered a carriage round and had Lillie taken home. She sent her own physician, Francis Laking, to see to her and called herself the following afternoon to find out how she was. She found Lillie still unwell, but not ill. She was pregnant.

Where and when Lillie's daughter was born remained a close-kept secret. Christened Jeanne Marie, the baby was placed in the care of Lillie's mother. Lillie did not want a child around to interfere with her pleasure-seeking way of life or with the stage career she had in mind now that her husband, having sold his yacht, his hunters and his house on the south coast in order to keep pace with her extravagances, had finally left her.

Just as the where and when of the baby's birth was a mystery, so was the tantalizing question of who was the father. The few who knew about the birth were inclined to favour Bertie—and he did not deny it.

EDDY AND GEORGIE

Winter still lingered in St Petersburg, with snow on the rooftops and slush in the streets, when Bertie and Alix arrived there in March 1881. But this time there was no skating; no gay sleigh-rides. The Russian capital was a city in mourning. Tsar Alexander II, after so many hair's breadth escapes, had been finally assassinated, his body torn almost in halves by a bomb.

Alix's sister, Minnie, was now Empress of Russia. As always in times of stress, she begged Alix to go to her.

Alix, when her sister's telegram arrived, wanted to go at once. But Queen Victoria would not give permission until Bertie managed to persuade her.

"We ought to go," he said.

Alix took with her only one lady-in-waiting, Charlotte Knollys, who was unmarried. There was no knowing what the situation in Russia would be and it would be unfair to take anyone with dependents, she said.

They found Minnie looking pale and ill in the aftermath of her father-in-law's death. She and Sasha, the new Tsar, had not yet moved into the vast, ornate and draughty Winter Palace, where the old Tsar had died, but were still living in their old home, Anitchov Palace on Nevsky Prospect. It was more comfortable, though that was not the only reason they stayed there. At Anitchkov, with trenches dug around it, venturing out only under close escort, they could be more easily protected.

Bertie and Alix, too, could not go out without escort. In the church of St Peter and St Paul they paid their respects to the remains of the dead Tsar. For Alix, it was a shattering experience. The funeral service, held under constant fear of a further attempt on the life of the new Tsar, was hardly less nerve-racking, and Bertie was heartily glad when, at the end of seven days, it was time to take his leave. But Alix did not go with him. Dutiful as always, ignoring both her own fears and the objections of her mother-in-law in England, she stayed on in St Petersburg to comfort her grieving and frightened sister.

More and more, though together in public, Alix and Bertie were living their private lives apart. Bertie was away a lot—in Paris, Cannes, Baden, Homburg (where, on one occasion, he revelled in a series of wheelbarrow races which invariably ended with the female occupants of the barrows being deposited on the grass in a state of disarray). In his absence, Alix retreated to Sandringham or went over to Denmark.

However, husband and wife were together at the Haymarket Theatre on 20th December 1881, to see Bertie's mistress, Lillie, make her stage debut in a charity matinee of *She Stoops To Conquer*.

She was "a great success", Bertie said, enthusiastically.

The theatre critic of *Punch* was less pleased. "Mrs Langtry is of too solid a physique for any light skittish movement," he wrote. "Her laugh, not yet being under control, appears forced and painful; and her action is as constrained and mechanical as that of any Eton sixth form boy on speech-day. Nevertheless, every entrance and exit was applauded frantically."

Squire Bancroft, who produced the play, knew when he was on to a good thing. He invited Lillie to join his regular company and early in 1882 she played the lead in *Ours*, a melodrama of the Crimean War. Bertie was in the audience on 28th January, having travelled up from Sandringham. He was in the audience

again in February. And again in March. He attended a late-night
supper party Lillie gave to celebrate the success of the play and
was often to be found at the five o'clock dinner parties she gave
for a select few guests before going to the theatre for the evening
performance.

Bertie had recently bought himself a new schooner of 216
tons, *Aline*. He was also dabbling in horse racing. A jumper
named Leonidas, bought on the advice of his friend, Marcus
Beresford, won the Military Hunt Steeplechase at Aldershot in
1880. Another—Fairplay—won the Household Brigade Cup at
Sandown. In an attempt to reduce his girth, he had taken up
both fencing and the new craze of lawn tennis, a fact which did
much to popularize the game.

For Alix, the year of 1882 was one of mingled joy and
heartbreak. That summer she said goodbye to Oliver Montagu,
the man whose companionship and obvious, if unspoken, love
had helped to offset the pain of Bertie's unfaithfulness. He
was off with others of the Household Brigade to fight in Egypt.
Bertie, loving uniforms as he did, still hankering for a military
life, wanted to go, too. But his mother would not have it.

"Impossible", she told him. His "rank and position" made any
such idea most "unwise".

So while others went off to fight, Bertie remained behind.
Taunts and cartoons in various European newspapers did nothing
to help his temper.

For Alix, the heartbreak of saying goodbye to Oliver
Montagu was offset, in part at least, by the return of H.M.S.
Bacchante with Eddy and Georgie on board, each with a writhing
blue and red dragon tattooed on one arm as a souvenir of Japan.
Eagerly, she welcomed them back to her arms. They were
children no longer, but young men, Georgie as bright and
robust as ever, Eddy dull and backward still. It had not yet
occurred to anyone that his backwardness might be due to a
degree of the same deafness which afflicted both his mother and
her mother. The girls too were growing up, shy and plain, often
ill—especially Toria—and largely uneducated. Alix taught them
music, but little else. She was more concerned about the boys,
proud of Georgie, worried by Eddy. But she continued to treat
them all, boys and girls alike, as children long after childhood
had been left behind. When Georgie was an eighteen-year-old

midshipman, she was still going to his bedroom each night to hear him say his prayers.

From the time of her first visit to England Alix had had a soft spot in her heart for Leo, the Queen's haemophilic son who had come to the harbour to greet her with his bouquet of flowers. At twenty-nine he was a child no longer and Alix was delighted when he found a girl to marry him, Princess Helen of Waldeck Pyrmont. They were married in April 1882. But theirs was to be but a short-lived happiness.

In March 1884, while his wife awaited the birth of their second child, Leopold injured his knee at Cannes. To any ordinary person, it would have been a minor mishap of little consequence. But not to Leopold. In twenty-four hours he was dead from a haemorrhage of the brain. Bertie, like Alix, was extremely upset and set off immediately for Cannes to bring his brother's body home.

"I could not bear the thought of his returning home without a relative to look after him in death as they had done so often in life," he wrote.

Bertie had patched up his quarrel with Randolph Churchill. He may not entirely have forgiven Churchill, but he had long been fascinated by his vivacious, American-born wife, Jennie. Now he began calling upon her at her home in Connaught Place. He met her too at house-parties to which they were both invited. He invited her to Sandringham, gave her small gifts of jewellery and wrote her letters beginning, *"Ma chère amie"*.

Bertie and Alix had been married now nearly twenty years, and birthdays and anniversaries seemed to come round with astonishing rapidity. Hardly were they back at Marlborough House after one Christmas at Sandringham, it seemed, than they were packing to return there for another. January 1885 was Eddy's coming-of-age. The small, weakly baby, prematurely born at Frogmore, was now a young man of almost poetic good looks, but backward still, except when it came to the ladies. There was an incident with a girl in Malta which reminded his grandmother, when she heard of it, of Bertie's early amorous escapade with Nellie Clifden.

If Eddy, her firstborn, was always something of a heartache to Alix, he was becoming more and more of a headache to Bertie. The idea of keeping him and Georgie together in the hope that some of Georgie's brightness might rub off on him clearly had not worked. Eddy was making no progress at all in the Navy. What to do with him? He wanted to go to Cambridge, he said. So to Cambridge he went though his father was fast losing patience with him.

In the spring of 1885, Bertie and Alix decided to take Eddy to Ireland with them. It was a trip Bertie himself was not at all keen to make. It may not have bothered him that Ireland, at the time, was in a state of even greater unrest than usual and that an organization calling itself the "United Irishmen" was offering a reward of 10,000 dollars for him, dead or alive. It did irritate him that he was expected to pay out of his own pocket for a trip from which, as he said, he did not expect "to derive any personal pleasure". But the Government was insistent.

Neither Bertie nor Alix, whatever their faults in other directions—Bertie's unfaithfulness, Alix's childishness—lacked personal courage. In Dublin, where Alix, elegant as always in a white gown with scarlet sleeves, was installed as a Doctor of Music at the university, they were offered a mounted escort when they drove through the streets. Bertie declined it. As it turned out, except for a few broken shop windows, Dublin was enthusiastically loyal.

But elsewhere it was a different story. The skull and crossbones was waved defiantly at them as their special train journeyed from Dublin to Cork and stones banged against the windows. At Mallow, instead of the planned reception committee, they were greeted by an angry mob. So threatening was the situation that they did not get off the train and it steamed out again leaving police and demonstrators battling on the station platform. As they drove through Cork in their carriage, fists were shaken, sticks brandished, they were pelted with onions and a miniature coffin landed almost in Alix's lap. Through it all she continued to smile her unchanging smile and Bertie obstinately refused to change or curtail the arranged programme.

Their problems with Eddy were still not at an end. Just as he had failed in the navy, so he flopped at Cambridge. Bertie, who had always hankered for a military career himself, thought a spell in the army might cure him. He arranged for Eddy to become a subaltern in the 10th Hussars. It was quickly clear that Eddy was no more suited to an army career than he had been to a sea-going life.

In many ways, even if Bertie did not realize it, Eddy was very like his father. Like him, he was sensual and pleasure-seeking. But even in pursuit of pleasure he lacked his father's flair. He also lacked Bertie's robust constitution and more and more the type of life he was leading began to affect his health.

So far, Georgie had given his parents no cause for worry or concern. He was twenty now and handsomely bearded, a full-blown naval lieutenant. Alix and Bertie were proud of his success. But both of them—Bertie because he was heavily pre-occupied in other directions and Alix because she still looked upon him as a child—failed to realize that their younger son was now a young man with all a young man's natural passions and desires.

Desire, in Georgie's case, took the attractive form of a young lady named Julie Stonor.

Julie's mother had been one of Alix's ladies-in-waiting. Since her death some three years earlier, Alix, tender-hearted and considerate as always, had often had Julie and her brother, Harry, to stay at Sandringham and elsewhere. So Georgie and Julie had seen a lot of each other. They had also, though Bertie and Alix may not have known this, been writing to each other while Georgie was away at sea.

Christmas 1885 found Julie again invited to Sandringham, accepted and treated almost as one of the family. But if Alix looked upon her as another daughter, Georgie did not regard her as simply another sister. And now came an emotional bombshell.

He was in love with Julie, he told his mother, and wanted to marry her.

Alix was torn between love for her son, a mother's natural desire for his happiness, and her strong sense of royal duty. She had nothing against Julie. On the contrary, she was very fond of the girl. But there were other considerations. After Bertie and Eddy, Georgie was next in line for the throne. If anything happened to Eddy, Georgie would have to step into his shoes. There was always an outside possibility that one day he might find himself King. And Julie, both a commoner and Roman Catholic, could hardly be Queen.

Torn as she was, Alix did what she always did in such

situations, what she had always done in the matter of Bertie's unfaithfulness. She acted as though the situation did not exist and hoped it would go away.

It was, as things turned out, perhaps the best thing she could have done. Neither encouraged nor opposed, Georgie's love for Julie gradually died a natural death and she married someone else. But while it lasted, it served to keep him free from the sort of temptations to which Eddy succumbed during those impressionable, emotional years of early manhood.

Eddy still remained the real problem and Alix and Bertie now came to the same conclusion about him that Queen Victoria had once come to over Bertie. What Eddy needed was the right sort of wife to keep him straight. They began looking round for a suitable princess

SILVER WEDDING

At half-past eleven on the morning of Saturday, 10th March 1888, Queen Victoria's carriage drew up outside Marlborough House. It was Bertie and Alix's silver wedding day and they were waiting to greet the Queen, now nearing seventy, as she climbed down from her carriage in the company of her daughters, Lenchen and Beatrice.

Bertie at forty-six was beginning to look his years. Alix, at forty-three, in grey and white, looked not only beautiful but surprisingly young. But, then, she always did. Indeed, out with her daughters, she was sometimes mistaken for their sister. Despite the heartache and worry caused by Bertie's constant philandering, it was as though she had somehow come to terms with life so that the passing years had no effect upon her. She looked that Saturday morning "more like a bride just married than a silver wedding one of twenty-five years", as Queen Victoria noted in her journal. But though she had beauty and style in plenty, there was perhaps, as there had always been, something lacking. Her sister-in-law Vicky may have put her finger on it when she said (in what was intended as a compliment): "I have known many women who pleased all men, but never one, like Alix, who has gained the good word of her own sex without either arousing or exciting jealousy."

The Prince of Wales
sporting a homburg—
the hat he helped to
make fashionable

(Left to right) Alix, her sisters Dagmar (Tsarina Maria Federovna) and Thyra (Duchess of Cumberland), and King Christian IX of Denmark

Queen Victoria had brought with her her silver wedding gift—appropriately, a silver loving cup. For Alix—"Quite a daughter to me," the Queen remarked—there was also a silver and diamond brooch fashioned in a design of oranges and orange blossom.

Gifts by the score poured into Marlborough House to commemorate their twenty-five years together. There were so many, in fact, that Bertie later had the idea of displaying them in a specially-built case in the centre of the plate room so that visitors could walk round them as they did the Crown Jewels in the Tower of London.

From their five children there was a silver statuette of her favourite mare for Alix and for Bertie a matching statuette of his favourite hunter. There was a silver casket from the group of middle-aged women who, as young girls, had been bridesmaids at the wedding. Alix's parents, who travelled from Denmark to join the celebrations, brought them tea and coffee services in silver gilt. Alix's brother, the King of Greece, sent them a gold punch-bowl. From Minnie in St Petersburg there was a diamond and ruby necklace for Alix.

But of all the gifts she received that day, the one which delighted Alix most was a diamond and ruby cross. This was her gift from Bertie and she felt as much in love with him as ever as he fastened it about her throat.

Cheering crowds lined the streets as they all drove to Buckingham Palace for lunch. The celebrations continued that evening with a dinner party at Marlborough House for which the Queen arrived with an escort of Life Guards. For dinner, Alix wore Queen Victoria's orange and orange blossom brooch in her hair. It suited her because she was "no longer an orange blossom but a full-blown orange", she joked.

It was, curiously enough, the first time Bertie's mother had dined at Marlborough House in all the twenty-five years her son and Alix had been married. A "most happy family", the Queen called it.

It was very much a family occasion and among those who sat down to dinner that night was Alix's long-time friend, the girl her mother had once called a flirt, Princess Mary Adelaide, the blonde, buxom, extravagant, impoverished Duchess of Teck. With her that evening, in addition to her husband, Franz, was her daughter, May, fast-approaching her twenty-first birthday, slim and tightly corsetted after the fashion of the day, tall with a high, tight hair-style which made her look even taller, a girl with twinkling blue eyes and a ready laugh which she herself sometimes thought of as "vulgar". A girl who was not only attractive but had brains and character. And it was perhaps that evening that it first crossed Bertie's mind that May was just the sort of girl Eddy needed for a wife.

A FAMILY QUARREL

Queen Victoria was as concerned as anyone over the question of a bride for Eddy. As she had once done for her son, she now drew up a list of possible princesses for her grandson. First names on the list were Vicky's youngest child, Margaret, and Affie's eldest daughter, Marie. Alix didn't care for Marie at all and neither Margaret nor Eddy were keen on their grandmother's idea that they should marry each other.

Eddy, like his father, preferred strikingly attractive girls—like Alix of Hesse with her glinting red-gold hair. Alix was another of Queen Victoria's many grandchildren, the daughter of the dead Princess Alice, Bertie's sister. But if Eddy fancied himself in love with Alicky, she was not in the least interested in him. At seventeen, she was already in love with someone else—Minnie's son, Nicky.

Where monarchies were concerned, Europe, at this time, was largely a family affair. Bertie's mother on the throne of England. His sister Empress of Germany. Alix's father King of Denmark; her brother King of Greece; her sister Empress of Russia.

Fritz—Vicky's husband—was already a dying man in March 1888, when he succeeded his father as Emperor of Germany. In little more than three months he was dead. Bertie was at Ascot when the news reached him. He and Alix went to Berlin for the funeral. Bertie's nephew, the "foolish and conceited" Willy, who had tried to bite the knees of his youthful uncles on Alix's wedding day, was now Emperor at the age of twenty-nine. The words "foolish and conceited" came from Alix, but Bertie was in wholehearted agreement.

In Berlin for the funeral, Bertie was perhaps tactless—a rare

thing with him. Willy was certainly arrogant. Bertie treated
Willy as a nephew, while Willy wanted to be treated as an
Emperor.

It was the beginning of a family quarrel which, in the end, was
to affect the history of Europe. But, initially, it seemed laughable
rather than dangerous. When Bertie went to Austria that
September to watch the military manoeuvres and go shooting
with Crown Prince Rudolf, Willy suddenly decided that he
would go to Vienna as well. His would be a state visit, he
informed the Austrian emperor, and he must be the only royal
guest present. Frightened of offending Willy, the poor Emperor
had the embarrassing task of asking Bertie to leave the country.
Bertie, by turns astonished, puzzled, indignant and furious, took
off for Rumania.

Suppressing her own feelings, Queen Victoria did her best to
effect a reconciliation between her son and grandson. The following year she invited Willy to Osborne. In keeping with his
ideas of grandeur, he arrived with an escort of twelve warships,
Bertie, too, tried to patch things up by making his nephew a
member of the Royal Yacht Squadron. Willy was pleased by
that, but still did not like his uncle—"an old peacock", as he
called him.

Queen Victoria was seventy that year of 1889 when her
grandson, Willy, visited Osborne with his twelve warships. But
she still seemed as tireless as ever, as busy a letter-writer as she
had ever been. Shortly before her seventieth birthday she went to
visit Bertie and Alix at Sandringham. It was her first visit there
since Bertie's illness and servants hurried round putting the clocks
to the correct time. Alix wanted no further complaints from her
mother-in-law on that score.

Bertie and Eddy joined the train at King's Lynn for the
remaining few miles to Wolferton, where an open landau was
waiting. The Queen sat facing forwards—"in order that I may be
better seen"—with Alix and Louise seated opposite as the landau
drove under the triumphal arch at the station entrance and up the
hill to Sandringham.

There was talk of Louise getting married. Lacking both her
mother's beauty and her father's joie-de-vivre, there was little
about the girl to attract a man of her own age and she was
content to settle for a friend of her father's, the wealthy Earl of

Fife—"MacDuff", Bertie called him—some eighteen years her
senior. MacDuff, that year, had rented the neighbouring Castle
Rising estate the better to pursue his suit and a few weeks later,
over lunch at Windsor, Bertie sought his mother's consent to the
match. The Queen kissed her plain-looking granddaughter and
wished her all happiness. Louise and MacDuff (now a duke) were
married a month later in the Chapel Royal. Princess May, who
thought it "rather strange" for a royal princess to marry one of
her grandmother's subjects, was one of the eight bridesmaids.

So one child had been safely steered into the harbour of
matrimony. But Eddy was still a problem. His advances to Alix
of Hesse rejected, he was now in love—or so he told his
mother—with Helene d'Orleans, the tall, beautiful, dark-haired
daughter of the Count of Paris. Almost inevitably, there were
snags—the political snag that Helene's father was Pretender to
the French throne; the religious snag that she herself was a
Catholic. Marriage between them was "utterly impossible",
Queen Victoria said. As with Georgie and Julie Stonor, Alix
hardly knew what to do for the best. Bertie was not over-
concerned. His own love-life was undergoing one of its not
infrequent transformations.

DAISY

Bertie was in his study, seated at the pedestal table he used as a
writing desk, when Frances Brooke, known to her friends as
Daisy, called to see him. The study had that snug, rather intimate
atmosphere that goes with wood-panelled walls and velvet
curtains.

Daisy and Bertie were no strangers to each other. He had
attended her wedding to Lord Brooke, heir to the Earl of
Warwick, and had signed the marriage register. She was twenty-
eight now, slenderly built and strikingly beautiful, with classic
features, dark blue eyes and an air of aristocratic arrogance.
Queen Victoria thought her "very fast".

Daisy was not only "fast" but at this time also a damsel in
distress—to Bertie, an irresistible combination. Prettily she confessed that she had been having an *affaire* with one of his close
friends, Charles Beresford, but the wretched man had been

"unfaithful" to her by continuing to sleep with his own wife, who was now pregnant. In a fit of pique, Daisy had written him an indiscreet letter which his wife had opened and passed on to her solicitor, George Lewis. She wanted the letter back.

Bertie's relationship with Lillie Langtry had cooled since she went on the stage and left for America. She was back now and he still saw her from time to time. But it was time for a change.

He knew George Lewis, the solicitor, a specialist at coping with the legal whims of husbands who had compromised themselves or wives who sought divorce. The man had once been a dinner guest at Marlborough House. So when Bertie demanded to be shown Daisy's letter, Lewis, unprofessional though his action was, handed it to him.

Bertie read it. Destroy it, he directed Lewis.

Even Lewis baulked at that. He would need Lady Beresford's permission, he said.

Bertie drove round to see Beresford's wife. To his indignant surprise, she refused to have the letter destroyed.

Furious, Bertie ordered her name struck from his guest list. Others, when they heard, similarly struck her from their guest lists.

Charles Beresford, far from being pleased at Bertie's attempts to retrieve Daisy's indiscreet letter, was furious when he learned what had happened. How dare the Prince of Wales insult his wife in this fashion?

His Irish temper thoroughly roused, he rushed round to Marlborough House and burst in on Bertie.

"Blackguard", he called him, advancing with clenched fists.

"Don't strike the Prince of Wales," Bertie cautioned him.

"Coward", sneered Beresford.

Beresford went off to command the cruiser *Undaunted* in the Mediterranean—and Bertie went to bed with Frances Brooke. He was as completely infatuated with her as he had once been with Lillie Langtry, parading her around in public as proudly and flamboyantly as he had once squired Lillie. They went to Paris together, where they climbed the Eiffel Tower and saw a "shameless" farce at the Palais Royal. As a token of his love, he gave her the gold ring his parents had given him on his confirmation in 1860. Encouraged by Daisy, Bertie also continued his social ostracism of Lady Beresford.

Alix, at this time, was less worried about Bertie than about Eddy, still begging to be permitted to marry Helene d'Orleans. Eddy was her favourite and she could refuse him nothing. Completely disregarding the political and religious objections to a match between Eddy and Helene, she now set in motion another romantic plot just as she had once done for her sister, Thyra.

In this, she had the willing help of her daughter, Louise, Duchess of Fife. Louise invited Helene to stay with her at Mar Lodge, the Fife home in Scotland, a ramshackle hunting lodge on the banks of the Dee. Alix invited herself and Eddy there at the same time. And in August 1890, Eddy and Helene became engaged. Lacking Queen Victoria's consent, it was, of course, an entirely unofficial engagement, but Alix's romantic plot had not yet run its full course.

In her more than twenty-five years as a daughter-in-law, she had come to know Queen Victoria well. Beneath that seemingly bleak, autocratic exterior beat a sympathetic heart, as Alix had good cause to know. It might be difficult to move her to laughter, but tears came easily enough to those old, fading eyes. If the two young people went to her themselves to plead their cause, she was unlikely to refuse them.

So, with Bertie away at the gaming tables of Homburg, Alix packed Eddy and Helene a picnic lunch and sent them off to see the Queen at Balmoral, and tell her of their engagement.

"We arranged it entirely between ourselves without consulting our parents first," Eddy told his grandmother, which was perhaps not the exact truth.

The gambit worked. The Queen, completely won over by the sight of two young people so obviously in love, constented to their engagement.

There still remained the stumbling block of Helene's religion. Helene herself offered to change it. But her father, when he heard, was furiously opposed to the idea.

Alix sought Bertie's advice. Only too eager to get his son married and off his hands, Bertie saw no reason why Helene should not remain a Catholic, as her father wished, provided the children of the marriage were brought up in the Church of England.

But the prime minister, Lord Salisbury, shook his head. It was "dangerous", he thought.

Helene, determined to marry Eddy, appealed to the Pope. But the Holy Father was not prepared to let any Catholic, even one as vacillating as Helene, stray from the fold. He agreed with her father that she must remain a Catholic.

Helene was heartbroken. Eddy, his father thought, was equally wretched. But not so wretched as to prevent him promptly pursuing another attractive young woman—Sybil, daughter of the Earl of Rosslyn—as soon as he realized that Helene was not for him.

TRANBY CROFT

September 1890, found Bertie heading north, as he always did at this time of year, for the St Leger race meeting at Doncaster. Among those who journeyed with him was Sir William Gordon-Cumming, a forty-two-year-old lieutenant colonel in the Scots Guards, a friend of Bertie's for ten years or more. Frances Brooke should have gone too, but at the last moment was called to the bedside of a dying relative.

On previous visits to the St Leger Bertie had usually stayed at Brantingham Thorpe, the home of his old friend, the sycophantic Christopher Sykes. But Sykes was now on the verge of bankruptcy, partly through the inordinate expense of friendship with Bertie, and in no position to entertain anyone. So Bertie went instead to Tranby Croft, the home of Arthur Wilson, a wealthy shipowner.

Bertie arrived at Tranby Croft, a Victorian mansion conceived in a style more suited to sunny Italy than rainy England, on 8th September. Around eleven o'clock that evening, after dinner, the members of the house party settled down for a game of baccarat. It was Bertie's favourite card game and he had brought with him his own set of counters, engraved with the Prince of Wales feathers. He was banker.

Play had not been long in progress when Wilson's son, a young man of twenty-two, turned to the player next to him and whispered: "By God, Berkeley, this is too hot. This man next to me is cheating."

The man next to him was Bertie's friend, Sir William
Gordon-Cumming.

"You must be mistaken," Berkeley Levett murmured back.
"It is absolutely impossible."

"Look for yourself, said Wilson.

Bertie dealt the cards for the next *tableau* or game. Watching,
Levett (as he was later to say in court) saw Gordon-Cumming
surreptitiously increase his stake from £5 to £15 by the addition
of two more counters after his side had won.

Three deals later Levett again saw Sir William increase his
stake, this time from £5 to £10, on a win.

"It is too hot," he whispered to young Wilson.

Later, when the others had gone to bed, Wilson told his
mother what had happened.

"For goodness sake. don't let's have a scandal here," she
begged.

Wilson also told his brother-in-law, Lycett Green, who in turn
told his wife, Wilson's sister.

Next day they all went to the races, where one of Bertie's
horses was a winner. That night, they again played baccarat after
dinner. Extremely embarrassed by the whole wretched business,
Berkeley Levett carefully avoided looking at Sir William
Gordon-Cumming as play progressed. But Lycett Green and his
twenty-six-year-old wife both (so they said later) saw Bertie's
friend increase his stake on different wins.

Two other members of the house party, Lord Coventry and
General Owen Williams, were now informed. They went along
to see Gordon-Cumming. Indignantly he denied the charge
made against him and asked to see Bertie.

To Bertie, he reitereated his denial: "I emphatically deny that I
have done anything of the kind insinuated."

"But what can you do?" Bertie asked him. "There are five
accusers against you."

"Something must be done," Sir William insisted.

What was done took the form of a rather curious document,
drawn up by Lord Coventry and General Williams:

"In consideration of the promise made by the gentlemen
whose names are subscribed to preserve silence . . . with regard
to my conduct at baccarat . . . I will on my part solemnly
undertake never to play cards again as long as I live."

Shown the document, Sir William at first refused to sign. It was tantamount to an admission of guilt, he protested. Finally, however, he did sign. The other men of the party, Bertie included, "subscribed" their signatures and Bertie took charge of the document which he sent to Marlborough House for safe keeping. The ladies concerned, Mrs Wilson and her daughter, Mrs Lycett Green, were not asked to sign, and Lycett Green, who did sign, had already told his father when he met him at the races.

With so many people involved, it could hardly be hoped that the matter would remain a secret. Nor did it . . . and in due course Sir William brought an action for slander against his five accusers, Lycett Green and his wife, young Wilson and his mother and Berkeley Levett.

The case lasted from 1st to 9th June 1891, and Bertie was subpoenaed to give evidence. The whole business worried him so much that he was almost ill. Alix again supported him as loyally as she always had done. His mother thought it "a fearful humiliation to see the future King dragged (and for the second time) through the dirt".

Bertie was in court every day except one, when he went to Ascot. It was indeed a "fearful humiliation" to hear his favourite game of baccarat described by Sir Edward Clarke, representing Gordon-Cumming, as "the most unintelligent mode of losing your money or getting somebody else's, I ever heard of".

"I take it nothing occurred to give you the smallest suspicion of his play?" Sir Edward asked Bertie when he was in the witness box.

"Nothing whatever."

He was about to step down again when a member of the jury intervened.

"Are the jury to understand that, as banker, Your Royal Highness saw nothing of these alleged malpractices?"

"It is not usual for the banker to see anything in dealing cards," Bertie replied, "especially when you are playing among friends. You do not for a moment expect anything of the sort."

"What was Your Royal Highness's opinion at the time as to the charges made?" the juryman asked.

"The charges appeared to be so unanimous that it was the proper course—no other course was open to me than to believe them," Bertie replied.

The jury was out only thirteen minutes before finding in favour of the defendants, a verdict which was hissed by some of those in court.

By its verdict the jury, in a sense, had vindicated Bertie's part in the whole unhappy business. Not everyone agreed. *The Times* waxed eloquent on the subject of his "questionable pleasures". The *Daily Chronicle* really lashed out at him:

> The readiness of the Prince of Wales to dispose of himself as a prize guest in rich but vulgar families where his taste for the lowest type of gambling can be gratified . . . has profoundly shocked, even disgusted, the people who may one day be asked to submit to his rule.

Queen Victoria wrote him a letter of recrimination and there was another, which he resented more, from his nephew, Emperor Willy. Bertie's mother urged him to send the Archbishop of Canterbury a public letter condemning gambling. This, to his credit, Bertie declined to do. It would be "hypocritical", he said.

A self-appointed committee of high-born ladies approached the Archbishop and asked him to speak to Bertie about the bad example he was setting. They were perhaps less concerned with his gambling than with some other aspects of his way of life. Young married women no longer had any standard of morality, they told the Archbishop, and girls "newly come out" were quickly corrupted; and at the heart of it all was "the Marlborough House set".

Finding all this furore distasteful and humiliating, Alix again slipped off to Denmark. She would be back in time to go to Sandringham with him as usual for his fiftieth birthday, she told Bertie.

Bertie was still infatuated with "darling Daisy"; still furious with Lady Beresford. His social ostracism of Beresford's wife intensified to a point where she felt she could no longer endure it. She was considering selling their London home and going abroad to live, she wrote to her husband. Taking a leaf out of Randolph Churchill's book, he wrote back threatening to drag the whole sordid business into the open.

Beresford's letter was passed on to Lord Salisbury, the prime minister, and another scandal seemed imminent. The gossip reached Alix in Copenhagen and she changed her mind about returning home. Instead, with Minnie and Sasha's forthcoming silver wedding as an excuse, she went off to stay with them at Livadia, a still unspoiled wilderness of vineyards and white-washed cottages on the shores of the Black Sea.

When Alix did not return in mid-October, as originally planned, Bertie went off to spend the weekend with Frances Brooke and her husband at Easton Lodge, their country home in Essex. But dalliance with Daisy was cut short by the arrival of a telegram from Sandringham. The house had been badly damaged by fire.

The blaze had started in one of the top-floor bedrooms. While servants rescued furnishings and paintings, estate workers formed a human chain to fight the fire with water from the lake. The estate fire brigade was also in action with its hand-operated pump. But all these efforts, though energetic, were too small. The whole of the top floor was soon ablaze and the roof timbers collapsed with a crash.

Despite the fire, despite Alix's continued absence, Bertie was determined to spend his birthday at Sandringham as usual. Carpenters and painters were put to work, but could achieve little in the time and tarpaulins still covered part of the roof when Bertie went there a week later for his birthday celebrations. Eddy and Georgie, now a commander in the navy, were with him along with Louise, their married sister. The other two girls, Maud and Victoria, were in Russia with Alix.

That November, while Bertie was at Sandringham and Alix still in Livadia, Queen Victoria had a special guest at Balmoral . . . Princess May.

There was no longer any question of Eddy marrying Helene d'Orleans. But he had to marry someone and settle down, his father insisted. Either that or he would be packed off to the Colonies, hopefully out of harm's way.

But who was he to marry? Why not Princess May, his father suggested. So May found herself summoned north to Scotland.

For ten days, with her brother, Dolly, lending moral support, she stayed at Balmoral with its chill draughts and largely un-heated rooms, its stiff and starchy atmosphere, while Queen Victoria assessed her suitability as a bride for Eddy and a future queen. The Queen found her a nice, quiet, cheerful girl "carefully brought up and so sensible", and pronounced herself well satisfied.

At Sandringham, Georgie seemed to be sickening for something and his father had had enough experience of typhoid to hazard a shrewd guess as to what it was. He promptly broke up the house party and hurried Georgie back to London, where royal physicians quickly confirmed his fears.

A telegram went off to Alix at Livadia. She packed at once and, travelling night and day, was back at Marlborough House, at her son's bedside, in 144 hours.

She found Georgie sweating and feverish, delirious and rambling. Worried and distraught, she nursed him as conscientiously as she had once nursed Bertie. She prayed for his recovery and her prayers were answered. By 3rd December Georgie was out of danger.

The idea that Eddy should marry Princess May delighted Alix. She had known the girl from birth and was fond of her, as she was of her mother, the Duchess of Teck. If Georgie was well enough, she and Bertie would go to Sandringham for Christmas as usual and after Christmas they would invite May and her parents to join them there. The time and setting would be right for Eddy to pop the question.

But Eddy, who now fancied himself as much in love with May as he had once been with Helene d'Orleans, could not wait until after Christmas. That same weekend that Georgie was pronounced out of danger found Eddy invited to a house party at Luton Hoo being given by the Danish minister, C. F. de Falbe. May was there too and during the ball which formed part of the festivities Eddy contrived to get her briefly alone in Madame de Falbe's boudoir.

Back from Balmoral, Queen Victoria returned from visiting the widowed and exiled Empress Eugénie on 5th December, to learn that her grandson was waiting to see her.

"I have good news, Gan-gan," he told her, excitedly. "I am engaged to May Teck."

The Queen was happy for him. Alix was delighted. Bertie was relieved. At least that was Eddy settled.

But the Beresford business was still far from settled, still threatening yet another scandal.

Charles Beresford, in answer to another appeal from his

ostracized wife, had come storming back to England with fresh threats. Bertie must apologize to Lady Beresford and make amends, he insisted. Either that or he would broadcast the details of Bertie's dissolute private life.

The prime minister was already involved. Now Queen Victoria was drawn in. Alix, whatever she may have felt about her husband and Frances Brooke, supported him loyally as always. She knew, as Bertie knew, as Queen Victoria knew, that the royal family could ill afford another scandal so close on the heels of the Tranby Croft affair.

Bertie was angry, indignant, obstinate, worried. So worried that he decided not to go to Sandringham that Christmas after all. Instead, he stayed at Marlborough House, trying to sort things out. But there was only one way out and in the end he had to take it. On Christmas Eve he sat at his writing table, penning the letter of apology to Lady Beresford her husband was so insistently demanding.

TRAGEDY AT SANDRINGHAM

Georgie was well again, if not quite his old robust self. The Beresford business was over and done with. Eddy was engaged to May and, hopefully, had put his days of dissipation behind him.

For both Bertie and Alix, things seemed much brighter when they set off from London at the end of December. They planned to see the New Year in at Sandringham and would stay on there to celebrate Eddy's twenty-eighth birthday on 9th January. His wedding day had been fixed for 27th February and May and her parents had been invited to join them at Sandringham for his birthday celebrations.

Just as it had been a hard, cold winter the year Eddy was born at Frogmore, so it was again a hard, cold winter that year at Sandringham. The ice on the lake was thick enough for ice hockey, though Bertie, no longer as young and energetic as he had once been, was content now to play goalkeeper. But his shooting parties were as big and elaborate as they had ever been. Both Eddy and Georgie went shooting with him, though Eddy was suffering from what seemed like the beginning of a bad cold.

Alix and May, too, had colds and Toria was already in bed with
'flu.

Eddy's birthday celebrations on 9th January did not go off as
well as had been hoped. It was still freezing hard and fresh snow
had fallen in the night. Eddy himself was not feeling at all well.
He got up and came downstairs to unwrap his gifts, then went
back to bed. "So tiresome", Bertie grumbled.

It was, everyone thought at first, no more than a minor
indisposition. As well to call the doctor though. To Alix's dismay,
the doctor diagnosed pneumonia of the left lung.

Alix was almost frantic. Next to Bertie, Eddy was the one she
loved most—and perhaps, seeing in him sometimes the young
Bertie she had first known, she loved him more. She was
constantly in his small, narrow, high-ceiling, bay-windowed
bedroom at the front of the house while he lay wrapped in the
skin of a freshly-killed sheep, designed to make him sweat. May
and Georgie, too, were frequent visitors, standing in the door-
way, talking to Eddy as he lay in bed.

Their visits were discontinued on the orders of the specialist
who was called in as Eddy's condition quickly became worse.
There were now nurses to look after him, but Alix still would
not leave him. She spent the entire night of 12th January in the
sickroom while Eddy tossed and turned, raving deliriously of his
army life, his grandmother Queen Victoria, and his lost love,
Helene d'Orleans. A telegram went off to Queen Victoria at
Osborne: "Condition v. dangerous".

Daylight came with Alix still at the bedside, wiping her son's
sweating forehead, soothing him. All that day she stayed there,
her face white and drawn. Bertie wandered restlessly in and out.
Alix whispered to him that she despaired of poor Eddy's life.

It was after midnight before she could be persuaded to leave
her sick son and go to another room. She lay down to rest on a
sofa. Hardly had she closed her hot, tired eyes than someone was
rousing her. She must come at once.

She hurried back to the sickroom, sitting again beside the bed,
mopping Eddy's hot, sweating face, trying her hardest to keep
calm, but with tears streaming down her cheeks.

Eddy tried to raise himself on his pillow.

"Who is that calling me?" he asked, deliriously.

"It is Jesus calling you," his mother replied, quietly.

Eddy tried to say something else, but the words were incoherent, uttered only with difficulty and accompanied by "a terrible rattle in his throat".

Bertie joined Alix at the bedside of their dying son. One by one, the rest of the family, including May, crowded into the tiny, cramped bedroom. For over six hours they stayed there, hot and suffocating, Alix's face mirroring her despair, Bertie, his head in his hands, sobbing loudly.

"Gladly would I have given my life for his, as I put no value on my own," he wrote to his mother after Eddy had died at half-past nine that morning.

Alix said less, but was perhaps the more heartbroken of the two. Weak, backward and dissolute though Eddy had been, he was her firstborn and merited the special kind of love mothers have for their firstborn. Her old friend, Oliver Montagu, journeyed to Sandringham to comfort her. Within a year, he, too, was to die.

Alix wanted Eddy buried at Sandringham beside the infant son who had lived barely twenty-four hours. But Bertie felt that the funeral should be at Windsor.

As the coffin was transported the two miles from Sandringham to Wolferton station, Bertie walked behind it. Eddy's death had had a profound effect on him and he looked ill. At Windsor he sobbed openly as the funeral service proceeded on a bitterly cold day. Alix, looking down from the shadowy closet from which her mother-in-law had once watched her wedding, was "the picture of grief", Queen Victoria noted.

But Bertie's nature, as his mother also noted, was not one to bear sorrow or life without amusement or excitement. Noticeably bitter, more irritable than before, he buried his grief in a fresh outburst of spending, planning a new wing for Sandringham, commissioning a new yacht to be called *Britannia*.

For Alix, life would never again be quite the same. "I have buried my angel today and with him my happiness," she wrote to her mother in Denmark. Like her mother-in-law, Queen Victoria, she began a period of mourning that was to last for years. Never again did she dress in the old, bright colours which had for so long been her hallmark. At Sandringham she kept Eddy's bedroom just as it had been when he was still alive and for years afterwards she continued to place fresh flowers on the pillow on which his head had last rested.

For a time, Bertie was quite worried by the change in Alix. What she needed, he decided, was a break, a period of peace and quiet. He borrowed a villa at Eastbourne from his old friend, Harty Tarty, now Duke of Devonshire, and took her there. Georgie went with them and they invited May, the dead Eddy's fiancée, to join them too. On 27th February, the day on which Eddy and May should have married, in a welter of emotion they gave her the wedding presents which they and the dead Eddy had bought for her.

From Eastbourne Bertie and Alix went to a hotel at Cap Martin on the Riviera. But for Bertie there was none of the usual gallivanting about. Instead, they kept themselves to themselves, going for long drives, walking alone together on the beach.

One day Bertie ran into an old friend. "Don't you find this sort of life rather dull?" his friend asked him.

"What on earth does that matter if it does the Princess any good?" Bertie retorted, sharply.

GEORGIE AND MAY

Thinking about it afterwards, no one was quite certain how the idea that Georgie should marry his dead brother's fiancée first originated. Perhaps it had its origins in those terrible hours when the two of them stood together by the bedside of the dying Eddy. Perhaps their feelings for each other blossomed and flowered at their subsequent meetings—at Eastbourne in February; at Cannes in March (May was there with her parents and George at Cap Martin with his); at Sandringham in December.

However the idea originated, however it blossomed, it was May's father, the Duke of Teck, who first put it into words, recalling how Alix's sister, Minnie, when her Tsarevitch fiancé died, had married his brother.

Just as Sasha had succeeded his dead brother as Tsarevitch so, Georgie, a likeable young man with an "inexpressible charm" which reminded people of his mother, now succeeded the dead Eddy as next in line of succession to the throne. It meant a big

(*Above*) 'Daisy'—Frances Countess of Warwick—with the Hon.
Maynard Greville in 1905; (*below*) 1909: King Edward VII's last
Derby. To the King's left are Beresford, his Master of the Horse,
and George, Prince of Wales

King Edward VII and Queen Alexandra

change in his way of life. He loved the navy and had risen to the rank of post-captain. Now, reluctantly, he relinquished his command of H.M.S. *Melampus* and said goodbye to the sea.

Queen Victora wanted him to marry as soon as possible. She suggested Affie's daughter, Missy—Princess Marie—as a suitable bride. But Missy turned him down and, instead, was quickly betrothed to Prince Ferdinand, heir-apparent to the throne of Rumania. George himself was not over-bothered, but his father was furious.

Between themselves, the Tecks—mother, father, brothers—talked of the possibility that May might marry Georgie. The idea was also now in Queen Victoria's mind and she talked with Georgie about it. But for Georgie, between him and May, the ghost of the dead Eddy still lingered.

Alix's reaction was mixed. She was very fond of May. But in the aftermath of Eddy's death, she now found herself drawn closer to Georgie in a new and strongly possessive mother-and-son relationship. She had no wish for it to end . . . as she knew it must if he married May.

As 1892 merged with 1893 Alix was still a long way from being her old self. A spring cruise of the Mediterranean might help. Bertie announced that he could not go with her; he had other plans. Alix neither minded nor cared. It was Georgie she wanted with her. Reconciled now to the idea that he would marry May, she knew this was perhaps the last opportunity she would have of getting her son all to herself.

Toria and Maud also went on the cruise, which took them as far as Athens where they visited Alix's brother, the King of the Hellenes. Georgie had still not fully made up his mind about marrying May and it was his Aunt Olga, the Queen of Greece, who helped him to do so. She knew May and liked her. "I'm sure she will make you happy," she told her nephew.

Leaving his mother and sisters to visit Italy on their own, Georgie returned to England, where his married sister, Louise, again played matchmaker as eagerly as she had once done for Eddy and Helene d'Orleans. She invited both May and Georgie to tea at her Richmond home, Sheen Lodge. Tea over, she urged Georgie to take May into the garden. It was 3rd May, a day of warm, bright sunshine, more like summer than spring. They

10—BAA * *

stood together by the lily pond. When they came indoors again they were engaged.

Queen Victoria was delighted, though it was no more than she had expected. Alix's feelings were mixed. "Poor Alix sent me a sad telegram," her mother-in-law noted. Closer to Georgie now than she had ever been while Eddy lived, Alix was sad "to think we shall never be able to be together . . . in the same way". Nor could she rid herself of Eddy's memory.

"Let me welcome you back as my dear daughter," she wrote to May. "God grant you all happiness here on earth which you so fully deserve—with my Georgie—which was alas denied you with my darling Eddy."

As the wedding day—6th July—drew near, Marlborough House was almost bursting at the seams with visiting royalties. Alix's parents, who had not long since celebrated their golden wedding, journeyed from Denmark. Minnie's son, Nicholas, was there, almost inseparable from Alicky. Bertie, as fussy as ever in the matter of dress, did not think much of Nicky's clothes and promptly sent him off to his own tailor, hatter and bootmaker to be rigged out afresh.

The wedding day was overpoweringly hot. Touched by the emotion of the occasion, Queen Victoria decided to wear her own wedding lace again—over black, of course—and her wedding veil. Taking the bride's mother with her, she drove to the Chapel Royal in her new glass state coach. As it turned out, they were the first to arrive and the Queen sat there lost in thought, her mind going back to her own wedding in that same chapel over half-a-century before.

The bridegroom arrived, accompanied by his father and Uncle Affie, all three in naval uniform. Then came May, with her father, her brother, Dolly, and her ten bridesmaids, among them Georgie's sisters, Victoria and Maud. She was in a wedding dress of white brocade with an interwoven design in silver of shamrocks, thistles and roses. On her head, reversed as a diadem, she wore the diamond necklace the Queen had given her for a wedding present. If the Queen's thoughts went back to her own wedding, who knows what Alix's thoughts were as she watched her surviving son marry the girl Eddy should have had. Whatever her thoughts, she kept them to herself, but the Queen could not help noticing that she looked very pale. More than pale—sad, her nephew, Nicholas, thought.

Georgie and May spent their honeymoon at Sandringham. They stayed not in the main house, but in the unpretentious, slate-roofed guest annexe which Bertie gave them as a wedding present and which was to be their future home. It was small, cramped and inconvenient, quickly permeated with the smell of cooking, but Georgie loved it.

Just as Vicky had once intruded upon Bertie and Alix's honeymoon at Osborne, so Alix now intruded upon Georgie and May. They had been married only thirteen days when she walked in with her two unmarried daughters, the lively Harry and the increasingly sharp-tongued Toria.

After that, she took to dropping in often. She was possessive of Georgie; critical of May. To Queen Victoria, May was "an excellent, good and useful wife . . . wonderfully wise and sensible". She hoped that May and George would "set an example of a steady, quiet life which alas is not the fashion these days". Alix did not always see her new daughter-in-law in quite the same rosy light. She did not always agree with the way May ran things. She interfered. Once, in May's absence, she even went as far as to have the furniture moved around in the drawing room. Georgie thought the result "much prettier". May, understandably, was less pleased.

Alix, those around her noticed, was becoming increasingly unpunctual, increasingly erratic, increasingly eccentric. She treated her unmarried daughters as unpaid companion-helps who were there to fetch this and carry that. With Eddy dead, Georgie married and Bertie still gallivanting around, she needed the reassurance of their company more now than ever and made not the slightest attempt to urge them towards marriage, a fact which more and more troubled Queen Victoria. In the end, the Queen spoke to Bertie about it.

The girls had no real desire to get married, he told his mother.

Whether they had or not, he was not really interested. The only 'girl' he was interested in was Frances Brooke, now the Countess of Warwick. He was constantly seen with her at the races, theatres, fashionable restaurants. He took her with him to Paris as he had once taken Lillie Langtry. When he was apart from her, he wrote letters to "My own adored little Daisy wife", as he called her.

For both Bertie and Alix, the one just turned fifty, the other approaching it, these were the middle years of marriage, the years when children marry and grandchildren are born and, occasionally, the sudden shock of a close friend, like Oliver Montagu, dying.

The same year in which Georgie married May, Louise gave birth to another daughter, Maud. The following year Georgie and May had their first child and Alix and Bertie their first grandson—"A fine, strong-looking child," Queen Victoria recorded happily.

May had gone to her parents' home, White Lodge, Richmond, for the confinement and there the baby was born on 23rd June 1894.

"My first joy since—" Alix began to say when her grandson was placed in her arms.

She stopped abruptly, but everyone knew she was thinking, as she so often did, of the dead Eddy.

The Tsarevitch Nicholas was again in England when the baby destined to be the Duke of Windsor was born. He had proposed to Alicky and she had accepted him. She was Queen Victoria's granddaughter and Nicky had come to Windsor to seek the Queen's approval. She gave it readily and Nicky and Alicky served as god-parents to her latest great-grandchild.

The baby was christened Edward Albert Christian George Andrew Patrick David, but ever afterwards he was to be called simply David. For Alix, his grandmother, the name Eddy had too many deeply painful associations.

PERSIMMON'S DERBY

October 1894 brought word from Minnie that Sasha was seriously ill. She begged Alix to go to her and on 30th October Alix and Bertie left London on the long journey to the Black Sea. They had got as far as Vienna when word reached them that Sasha had died.

They reached Livadia on 4th November to find everything in a state of confusion. Sasha's body had not yet been embalmed

though Nicky, their twenty-six-year-old nephew, had been proclaimed Tsar in succession to his father. It was a job he did not
want. "I know nothing of the business of ruling," he told them.

Alix did her best to console the widowed Minnie. At night
the two sisters again slept together as they had once done in
childhood.

With others of the family, Bertie and Alix made a twice-daily
pilgrimage to pray for the soul of the dead Tsar and kiss the dead
lips as he lay in his coffin. Bertie's fifty-third birthday passed
almost unnoticed.

With them, on that twice-daily pilgrimage, went Alicky of
Hesse. She and Nicky had planned to marry the following
spring, but now Nicky wanted to marry at once.

On a bright, clear day, with the sea sparkling, the purple-
draped coffin of the dead Tsar was taken to Sevastopol, where
Cossacks lifted it aboard the funeral train. Alix, Bertie and the
others climbed in after it and slowly it chugged its way towards
distant St Petersburg, with the weather turning from Riviera-
like sunshine to biting cold. In St Petersburg, where Georgie
joined his parents, cold winds swept along the boulevards and
there was slush underfoot. Every day there was another look
at the dead Sasha in his still-open coffin and another service
in the candle-lit cathedral, oppressive with the smell of
incense. Not until 19th November after a final service lasting
three hours, was the body at last laid to rest. Minnie broke down
completely.

A week later, on Minnie's birthday, Nicky and Alicky were
married in the chapel of the Winter Palace. Alix thought her
namesake looked "too wonderfully lovely" in an old-fashioned
court dress of silver brocade with an ermine-trimmed train.

On 2nd December, the day following Alix's fiftieth birthday,
Bertie and Georgie left for home. For two months more Alix
stayed on in St Petersburg, comforting her widowed sister. In
gratitude, her nephew, the new Tsar, knowing of her passion for
Fabergé, gave her one of the master jeweller's latest creations, a
small gold pot in which bloomed a crystal flower with a
diamond centre.

Alix returned home to find Bertie enthused over his prospects
for the new racing season. Eight years of racing had so far
brought him only £5904 in winnings, a miserable return. But

he now had a dozen horses in training at Newmarket, including Persimmon for whom there were high hopes.

Lillie Langtry, now a wealthy actress with her own yacht, a string of racehorses and a house in Pont Street, had what she called "a cottage" not far from Newmarket. In fact, Regal Lodge was a substantial brick-and-timber establishment with its own stables and a staff of twenty.

Daisy Brooke was still Bertie's mistress. All the same, he liked to look in on Lillie whenever he was in Newmarket. He still went to her first nights; still saw her from time to time, by either accident or design, in Paris, Baden, Homburg. Plumper now than she had been, she could still twist him round her little finger. When Bertie, financially hard pressed as nearly always, decided to close down the Egerton House establishment, his trainer, Richard Marsh, appealed to Lillie to intervene.

She invited Bertie to Regal Lodge, and raised the matter with him.

"My racing expenses must be cut down," he told her. He would save "hundreds a year" by closing down Egerton House and putting his horses elsewhere.

They sat together in Lillie's boudoir, eating peaches and drinking hock. By the time he left Bertie had changed his mind about closing down Egerton House.

Bertie's optimism, that year of 1895, proved justified. By the end of the season Florizel II had won six races, including the Gold Vase at Ascot. Persimmon had his first victory, the Coventry Stakes at Ascot, and followed it up by winning the Richmond Stakes at Goodwood. By the end of the season Bertie had won £8281.

He was still the same old Bertie, as quickly restless, as easily bored, as unfaithful as ever. The October of that year found him spending only four days at Marlborough House and a further two at Sandringham. The rest of the month was spent visiting Newmarket (twice), Easton Lodge (to see Daisy), the Duchess of Marlborough, Lord William Beresford, the Vyners at Newby Hall and an M.P. friend near Leeds. But not all of his time was spent in pursuit of pleasure. He was doing more minor royal chores, as president of this or patron of that, opening congresses, making speeches, popping in and out of the House of Lords.

Alix was still left largely to her own devices. She took up photography and filled her mornings also with painting and embroidery. In the afternoons she visited schools of art and hospitals, presenting prizes, opening wards, laying foundation stones. In the evenings she drove in the park. On Sundays she went to church—to Christ's Church in Down Street, All Saints in Margaret Street or St Anne's in Soho.

The year brought her and Bertie another grandson. At York Cottage on 14th December, the anniversary of the Prince Consort's death, May gave birth to a lusty, eight-pound baby boy. Because of the day on which he was born, the baby could hardly be called other than Albert—which was quickly shortened to Bertie, like his grandfather—and he was accordingly christened Albert Frederick Arthur George.

But if she was gaining grandchildren, Alix was equally losing her own sons and daughters—Eddy dead, Louise and Georgie married. And now Harry, as Maud was nicknamed.

She became engaged to her cousin, Prince Charles of Denmark, second son of Alix's brother, Freddy. Their marriage in the Chapel Royal in July 1896 was a quiet affair by royal standards and off they went to live in Copenhagen. Bertie gave them another of his houses at Sandringham, Appleton House, for a wedding present.

Now only Toria was left to keep her mother company and Alix clung to her desperately and selfishly. The result, for Toria, was to be long, lonely years of frustrated spinsterhood. She fell in love with Sir Arthur Davidson, but was sharply informed that marriage to an equerry was out of question. Later, the widowed Lord Rosebery wanted to marry her and Toria was more than willing. But that romance, too, was stamped on by her parents.

Bertie's high hopes for his horse, Persimmon, seemed doomed to disappointment. He was beaten by Leopold de Rothschild's St Frusquin in the Middle Park Plate and an abscess kept him out of the Two Thousand Guineas, which also went to St Frusquin. Then came Derby Day. St Frusquin's previous victories found him an odds-on favourite. Persimmon was 5–1 against.

Tense and excited, Bertie watched as Bay Ronald led at Tattenham Corner with St Frusquin in second place and Persimmon hard on his heels. St Frusquin took the lead with Persimmon still following. Bit by bit, eating up the ground with a long, raking stride, Persimmon narrowed the gap. With a hundred yards to go the two horses were neck and neck.

When Bertie's purple and red racing colours were first past the post it was as though the whole of the Downs went mad. The cheers were deafening. Hats—toppers and cloth caps alike—were thrown into the air, many to be lost to their owners for ever. Almost bursting with pride, Bertie strode out to lead in the royal winner.

Persimmon went on to win the St Leger and the Jockey Club Stakes, and the end of the season found Bertie second in the list of winning owners with over £28,000 in prize money. He spent much of it on further improvements to his beloved Sandringham, including a new range of hot-houses.

There were more victories for Persimmon the following year, more prize money for Bertie, £9285 from the Eclipse Stakes and £3380 from the Ascot Gold Cup.

At Ascot, where the dining room of his pavilion was draped with striped white and blue linen to resemble the inside of a tent, Bertie had Frances Brooke with him to witness Persimmon's triumph in the Gold Cup. But she had left by the time Lord Marcus Beresford, who managed Bertie's Sandringham stud, came over to him. He had a very great favour to ask, he said.

"Anything," said Bertie, still intoxicated by the excitement of Persimmon's victory. "I should be delighted to grant it."

To his amazement, Marcus Beresford burst into tears.

Through his blubbering he stammered out his request. Could he bring his brother Charles over to congratulate His Royal Highness on Persimmon's win?

Bertie was trapped. He had not spoken to Charles Beresford since the Christmas of 1891 when he had been compelled to write that humiliating letter of apology to Lady Beresford.

"I will never forgive or forget," he had said at the time.

But he had just given his word to Marcus and there was nothing he could answer but "Yes".

Marcus dried his tears and hurried off to collect his brother. Charles approached hat in hand. The two men, the Prince of Wales and his onetime friend, shook hands. For a few minutes they stood talking about the racing. Then Bertie turned away and they parted again.

DIAMOND JUBILEE

It was 1897 and Queen Victoria, her eyesight failing but her memory as good as ever, had been on the throne now for sixty years—longer than any other monarch in British history. It was not an occasion to be passed without celebration though the Queen herself was not one for pomp and ceremony. And if there must be pomp and ceremony, then the public must also be content for her to appear in her long-running role as the black-garbed widow of Windsor. It was left to Alix to try to persuade her otherwise.

As a result of Alix's persuasion, her mother-in-law presided over a celebration dinner in the Supper Room at Buckingham Palace with the front of her dress embroidered in gold, and diamonds sparkling at her throat and in her cap. For Queen Victoria, it was a considerable concession. And for the celebration drive through London on 22nd June her black silk dress was relieved by panels of grey and her bonnet decked with creamy-white acacia.

The capital was gay with flags and bunting, Venetian masts and triumphal arches. Bertie had the outside of Marlborough House decorated with his mother's VRI cypher and his own Prince of Wales' feathers. The new marvel of electric light added to the brightness of it all, though the lamps beading the floral arches in St James's Street short-circuited when Alix pressed the button which should have illuminated them.

The boom of guns in Hyde Park heralded the Queen's departure from the palace on a day of brilliant sunshine. Ahead of her snaked a long line of troops from all parts of her vast empire: Lifeguards and Dragoons, lancers from Australia, cavalry from New Zealand, Sikhs, Cypriots, Dykas, Hausas, Fijians with red-dyed hair. So long was the procession that it was already passing the palace as the Queen sat at breakfast. All this in honour of a small, grim-looking little old lady, her face flushed with emotion as she clutched the sunshade of Chantilly lace presented to her by the House of Commons. Alix, in lace-trimmed mauve, her bonnet decked with mauve flowers, and Lenchen sat facing her. Bertie, looking plumper than ever in his field-marshal's uniform, cantered along at the side of the carriage.

To Alix, the roar of the crowd was muffled and distant. She was now so deaf that she could hear voices of only a certain pitch. To make matters worse, there were sometimes noises in her head. She seldom spoke of it, and never to Bertie. Only in May, her daughter-in-law, did she sometimes confide. Understandingly, May, when talking to Alix, was careful always to turn towards her so that she could lip-read what was said.

But Queen Victoria, though her eyesight might be failing, was far from deaf. As the crowd roared its loyalty, tears of emotion glistened in her eyes.

"They are kind—so kind," she murmured.

All at once the tears spilled down her cheeks. Alix reached out and took her hand.

Determined that the feasting and celebration should not be solely for the aristocracy, Alix had been working for months past on a plan for a huge celebration dinner for the poor of London—over 300,000 of them. Church halls and meeting places were rented all over London and an army of helpers recruited. Alix herself visited as many of the dining places as possible, Holborn, Clerkenwell and the People's Palace in Mile End Road where 1600 crippled children gave her a warm reception. Bertie went with her. He had his own charity project—the Prince of Wales Hospital Fund. He hoped to raise £100,000 and ended up with double that figure.

ENTER ALICE

Alix and Bertie were spending a weekend at Chatsworth as house-guests of Lottie and Harty-Tarty. It was January 1898, and the day's mail brought them each an unexpected letter.

Over the past year or so Bertie's passion for Frances, Countess of Warwick, had cooled considerably. She was as beautiful and young-looking as ever, as Alix was beautiful and young-looking, but had lost much of the vivacity and brashness which first attracted him to her.

Loss of Bertie's love may not have been over-important to Daisy, but she was concerned about the special place in society she had enjoyed during her years as his mistress. That she did not want to lose.

So she wrote to Bertie, a tender, touching letter of renunciation. A clever letter. Reading it, he felt a quick surge of emotion. He did what Frances, knowing him so well, had guessed he would do. He hurried along to show it to Alix.

Like Bertie, Alix was deeply stirred—so moved that tears started in her blue eyes. She too had had a letter from the Countess of Warwick, she told him.

Both letters said much the same thing. Her association with the Prince of Wales, Frances wrote, had been no more than platonic for some time past. She was deeply sorry if anything she had done had caused Alix to feel badly towards her; her actions, of course, had always been much magnified by unkind gossip. But she knew the Princess of Wales to be a noble and generous person who would not bear her malice and she begged Bertie not to withdraw his friendship from her.

Could she find it in her heart to forgive the Countess of Warwick, Bertie asked Alix.

She could.

"Will you receive her, then?"

Again Alix agreed and Bertie hurried back to his own room to write to Daisy.

"The end of your beautiful letter touched me more than anything," he wrote. "How could you, my loved one, imagine that I should withdraw my friendship from you?"

He visualized his wife and his ex-mistress becoming "quite good friends". They could perhaps work together for some philanthropic cause, he suggested. But Alix was not prepared to go quite that far. Asked to become president of a charity with which Frances was associated, she not only declined but had May, her daughter-in-law, do likewise.

With Daisy gone, Bertie's blue eyes roved round for a replacement. He found her at Sandown races.

He was on his way to the paddock when he ran into an acquaintance, Jack Leslie. With Leslie was Alice Keppel, wife of the Hon. George Keppel, brother of Lord Albemarle. At twenty-nine, Alice was exactly the sort of young woman Bertie liked best—voluptuous, vivacious, with chestnut hair, turquoise eyes, an alabaster complexion and a loud, bold voice.

Leslie introduced them. Captivated, Bertie insisted that Mrs Keppel must accompany him for the rest of the day.

Within days, he was calling on Alice at her London home when her husband was out. Within weeks she had become his mistress and had taken Daisy's place as a favoured house guest at those country mansions where Bertie spent his weekends.

Alix knew all about it, of course. Her attitude was one of resigned acceptance. She was sometimes cold and offhand towards Alice, sometimes openly jeering, but mostly, because there was nothing else she could do, she accepted her, inviting her to Marlborough House, to Sandringham, and aboard the royal yacht. In one way she benefited. Alice, she soon found, could calm Bertie's increasingly erratic temper when no one else could.

That same year also brought Bertie another new feminine friendship. Agnes Keyser was very different from Alice Keppel—older, unmarried, handsome enough to attract Bertie, strong enough to dominate him as Alix never could. With the outbreak of the Boer War, Agnes wanted to set up a hospital for wounded officers. Bertie persuaded some of his friends to provide the necessary finance and the outcome was what was later known as King Edward's Hospital for Officers. For the twelve years until his death in 1910 Bertie shared himself between Alice in Portman Square and Agnes in Grosvenor Crescent.

He was, at this time, again in financial difficulty. Extravagant and generous as he was, he was often pressed for money. Now the extra entertaining he had done to celebrate his mother's Diamond Jubilee added to his problems.

That he had managed to scrape by over the past ten years had been due in no small measure to the advice received from Baron Maurice de Hirsch. The two of them had met in Paris and quickly struck an unspoken bargain. Hirsch advised Bertie on his investments. Bertie, in return, introduced him into high society. Now Hirsch was dead. And almost his last service to Bertie was to introduce him to Ernest Cassel, another financial genius. But even Cassel could not immediately put Bertie's rocky finances on a firm footing. Some economies had to be made. Bertie sold his racing yacht *Britannia*.

The autumn brought word that Alix's mother was dying. She must go to her. But Bertie could not go with her. He had fallen down one of the spiral staircases at Waddesdon while staying with Ferdinand de Rothschild and fractured a knee. In other ways, too, his health was no longer good and Alix was worried about leaving him. It was in a very torn state of mind that she set off for Denmark with Georgie for company.

The death of her mother on 29th September touched her deeply—"No words can describe my sorrow." She was concerned too for her father and arranged with her sisters, Minnie and Thyra, that the three of them should each stay with him in turn. She could hardly bring herself to leave him and lingered so long that Georgie became impatient to get home and Bertie wrote that he missed her.

ATTEMPTED ASSASSINATION

It was 1900, the first year of a new century—a year in which Bertie's brother, the heavy-drinking Affie, was to die of heart trouble. "My brother and I were devoted to one another," Bertie wrote sadly to a friend. Vicky too was dying (of cancer), though she lingered in the end a few months longer than their mother. It was a year in which Bertie was to win the Grand National with Ambush II and the Derby with Diamond Jubilee. It was a year when Britain was at war with the Boers. Bertie launched a fund to help the wives and families of British troops and Alix turned the cottage hospital at Sandringham into a convalescent home for wounded officers. With the help of Sir Thomas Lipton, she also organized a hospital ship to sail for South Africa. It was named *Princess of Wales* and she took Bertie to the docks to see over it. She arranged for twelve nurses from the London Hospital to sail with it, the start of what was later to become Queen Alexandra's Imperial Nursing Service.

Throughout much of Europe, feeling against Britain was running high. In Germany, nephew Willy was openly on the side of the Boers. In France, too, there was unveiled hostility towards Britain. So much so that Bertie, much as he loved Paris, decided not to attend the international exhibition there, the first time he had missed it in eighteen years. He also cancelled his customary jaunt to the Riviera with Alice Keppel. Instead, when Alix set off for Denmark to visit her widower father, he went with her.

They travelled by way of Brussels and it was ten minutes to five on the afternoon of 4th April when their train pulled in to the Gare du Nord.

They had forty minutes to wait. Bertie got out on to the platform and took a turn up and down to stretch his cramped legs.

It wanted only a minute or so to half-past five when he climbed back aboard and sat down again beside Alix. The window on the platform side of their compartment was open.

The train began to pull out. Suddenly there was a commotion on the station. A young Belgian student named Sipido, little more than a boy, raced across the platform and jumped on to the footboard of the compartment. There was a pistol in his hand.

He levelled it at Bertie and Alix through the open window and squeezed the trigger. There was a harmless click as the weapon misfired. Again he pulled the trigger and again there was only a click.

His hand trembling, the boy tried yet again. This time a shot rang out, but the jolting of the train sent it wide of its mark.

The boy steadied the pistol and to Alix, almost face to face with him through the open window, it seemed that he was aiming at her rather than Bertie.

A second shot rang out.

"I saw him coming straight at us and felt the ball buzzing across my eyes," Alix said afterwards.

The bullet passed directly between her and Bertie and buried itself harmlessly in the thick plush upholstery of the carriage.

Bertie said something in French which sounded like "Bad shot." He displayed considerable "courage and fortitude", Alix thought.

On the platform, the stationmaster and others rushed forward, grabbed the boy and pulled him from the footplate as the train came to a standstill again. Nerves were tense and tempers ran high. The would-be assassin, who turned out to be no more than fifteen, would have been badly beaten if Bertie, leaning out of the window, had not intervened.

"It was a narrow shave indeed which God alone mercifully averted," Alix wrote to Georgie, when they arrived later in Copenhagen. "Thank God I was with Papa and shared the danger in full. It would have been much worse hearing of it afterwards."

PART FIVE

King and Queen

THE POSTPONED CORONATION

It had seemed to some, at times, that Queen Victoria would live for ever. But now, in the January of 1901, her eyesight and her power of speech both failing, her children and grandchildren around her, she lay dying in her canopied bed at Osborne.

A coded telegram from Lenchen that their mother had had a stroke brought Bertie hurrying from Newmarket. That was on 19th January. The next day, to his annoyance, he had to return to London to greet his nephew Willy who had travelled from Germany to pay his last respects to his dying grandmother. Together, the nephew and the uncle who so disliked one another journeyed to Osborne. They found the once indomitable Queen growing steadily weaker, hardly able to speak, sometimes unconscious.

Awareness and recognition flickered briefly in the fading eyes.

"Bertie," she said, stretching out her matchstick thin arms. Weeping, he bent over her and held her thin, fragile body.

That night a storm broke over the Italian-like mansion where the Queen lay dying. The rain lashed down and the wind gusted in from the sea. But with the coming of daylight it had blown itself out.

The family huddled round the canopied bed. The Queen's pet Pomeranian, Turi, was curled up at her feet. Two clergymen intoned prayers. Outside the gates of Osborne a crowd of people waited for news of the Queen's death. Darkness came again and still the Queen lingered.

Then at half-past six that day—22nd January—she died in the arms of her grandson, Willy.

News of her passing was announced to the crowd waiting beyond the gates. Reporters jumped on their bicycles and pedalled frantically towards Cowes to be first with the news.

"Queen dead! Queen dead!" they yelled to people they passed on their way.

It was Willy who measured the Queen for her coffin. He wanted to lift her into it, too, but Bertie and his brother, Arthur, Duke of Connaught, insisted that the prerogative was theirs.

For ten days the body of the little old lady who had been Queen for close to sixty-four years lay in state, her lace wedding veil over her face and her white widow's cap covering her head, as she had directed long ago. Death, she had always believed, would see her reunited with her beloved Albert.

Bertie, at the age of fifty-nine, mentally depressed and physically exhausted, was now King. Alix, at fifty-six—and looking twenty years younger—was Queen.

But until the old Queen's body was finally laid to rest beside Albert's in the mausoleum at Frogmore she would not be addressed as "Your Majesty".

"There can be only one Queen until after the funeral," she said.

Bertie, by contrast, was irritated when he boarded the *Victoria and Albert* to find the royal standard flapping at half-mast.

"Why?" he wanted to know. "The Queen is dead, Your Majesty," came the stammering explanation.

"But the King lives," Bertie retorted.

Contrary to his dead mother's wishes, he did not take the title of King Albert Edward—a combination of names he had always disliked. He would be plain King Edward, he insisted.

Said *The Times*: "We shall not pretend that there is nothing in his long career which those who respect and admire him would wish otherwise." But he had "never failed in his duty to the throne and the nation".

Husband and wife made their first public appearance together as King and Queen at the state opening of Parliament. Bertie insisted that the extra throne which had been constructed for Alix should stand squarely beside his own. He might be unfaithful to her, but he respected the position she now occupied as Queen and insisted that everyone else should do the same.

They sat holding hands, Bertie in uniform, Alix wearing a black gown under her ermine-lined cloak, pearls in her ears and at her throat. She felt tense and nervous. But gradually, as her eyes wandered round the packed confines of the House of Lords, her tension evaporated. She nodded to someone she knew; then to someone else. There was something of a scrimmage at the bar of the House as members of the Commons jostled for the best positions. Alix, watching it, smiled. For the first time in many years, she was beginning to enjoy herself again.

As Queen, as those close to her were quick to realize, she was very different from the person she had been as Princess of Wales.

Hitherto, she had been easy-going in the extreme, deferring always to others, seemingly content to do always as she was told or advised. But now it was as though something of her dead mother-in-law had rubbed off on her. She would be called Queen, she insisted—not Queen Consort. For her coronation she would wear what she liked and not what others thought she should wear. She would personally select her ladies-in-waiting and would not have anyone around her simply because of some so-called claim or precedence.

"As Princess of Wales," she said, bluntly, "I was never permitted to do as I chose. Now I shall do as I like."

And she did. The year following his accession Bertie refused to let her accompany him on his birthday procession. Alix did not argue. But as soon as he had left she ordered round her own carriage and tagged on behind as the procession moved off along the Mall.

From childhood she had always been unpunctual. For her to be twenty or thirty minutes late for an appointment or a meal was nothing. But now, almost as though she did it at times deliberately to irritate Bertie, she became even worse, lingering in her boudoir while Bertie paced impatiently back and forth or sat drumming his fingers with impatience.

"It will do him good," she said on one occasion when she was told the King was waiting for her.

On one occasion she and Bertie were due to receive a number of deputations at ten-minute intervals starting at noon. Bertie, as always, was ready on the dot. But not Alix. One by one, the various deputations arrived and were shown into various rooms to wait their turn. Half-past twelve came, then quarter to one, and still Alix was not ready. It was ten minutes to one when she finally put in an appearance.

"Am I late?" she asked unconcernedly as she walked into the room.

Bertie could not trust himself to speak. Red in the face, almost bursting with anger and indignation, he stalked out.

At first, Alix obstinately refused to move into Buckingham Palace. She much preferred her old home with its comfort, its cosiness and its memories, she said.

Leaving Marlborough House "will finish me", she wrote to Georgie. "All my happiness and sorrows were here, nearly all my children were born here, all my reminiscences of my whole life are here."

With Bertie, her arguments were less nostalgic, more practical. The rooms allotted to her at the palace would not hold half the beautiful things she had collected around her at Marlborough House, she said.

Bertie himself had little liking for the palace with its drab paintwork and its dust-sheeted furnishings. "The Sepulchre", he called it.

"But it is a duty and necessity to live there," he told Alix.

They argued too over Windsor, where the Prince Consort's hat, gloves and cane still lay on the table in the room which had been his and where photographs and other mementos of John Brown still adorned the dead Queen's room.

"Those can go," Bertie ordered, pointing to the souvenirs of Brown.

Alix wanted to occupy the state rooms at Windsor. Bertie thought his parents' rooms much more comfortable, and Alix's deafness caused him to adopt his most penetrating voice as he stumped from room to room with his walking stick as though he was still out in the gardens. To an outsider, it might have sounded as though they were quarrelling furiously, but May, who was with them, knew otherwise. To her, it was highly amusing.

Finally Alix gave way over Windsor as she had done over the palace. There was a great sorting out of the relics of Queen Victoria's long life. At both castle and palace, a small army of carpenters, plumbers, painters was set to work to renovate and decorate. Electric light was installed and somehow Alix managed to squeeze in all her "beautiful things". Marlborough House was handed over to Georgie and May. May thought it "filthy dirty" and planned to redecorate, much to Bertie's indignation. He offered them Osborne House, too. But this Georgie refused. He could not afford the upkeep, he said.

Georgie might opt out of those things he felt he could not

afford. Bertie either couldn't or wouldn't. Parliament voted him £450,000 a year. There was another £60,000 from the Duchy of Lancaster and yet another £60,000 for Alix. It was still not enough and they tried to make economies, reducing the palace staff from 350 to 300.

Bertie turned to Ernest Cassel, who proferred sound financial advice if nothing more. Bertie was grateful. He made Cassel a Privy Councillor, gave him a knighthood and stood as godfather to his granddaughter, Edwina.

Overweight as he was, measuring some 48 inches round the waist, Bertie no longer played tennis and ice hockey tired him. He played bridge instead of baccarat and decided to take up golf. A ten-hole course was designed at Sandringham with wicker hurdles where the bunkers would be. But the hurdles, Bertie found, got in his way and he had most of them removed. When the time came to construct the actual bunkers, only two hurdles remained.

Bertie now had monarchy to occupy him in addition to all else. Alone more than ever, Alix felt she could not bear to be parted from Georgie, due to leave soon with May for an eight-month tour of Australia, South Africa and Canada.

She appealed to Bertie and he agreed that the tour should be cancelled. But the Government thought otherwise and on 16th March Georgie and May set sail in the liner *Ophir*.

Alix and Bertie went to Portsmouth to see them off. Georgie was as upset at leaving his mother as she was at parting from him. They clung to each other, both in tears. Bertie, too, was upset and had to choke back a sob while proposing a toast to Georgie and May at a farewell luncheon in the ship's dining room.

Above the swing cot in Georgie's cabin hung a picture of his mother with her first grandson, David. Above the sofa in his sitting room hung another picture of her, lovingly inscribed "Old Motherdear".

For her part, Alix had the consolation that Georgie and May had left the children—there were now four of them, David, Bertie, Mary and Henry—with her. She spoiled them abominably, as grandmothers will, keeping them up late and interrupting their lessons to take them on surprise outings.

Eager to move with the times, Bertie had electric light

installed at Sandringham as well as the palace. He bought himself
two cars, a Renault and a Mercedes. The year of his accession he
and Alix travelled to Sandringham for the first time by car. Alix
loved it. She found it an exhilarating experience to rush along at
speeds up to fifty miles an hour when the road was clear, though
the approach of a corner would find her poking the chauffeur in
the back as a sign to slow down.

She wanted to travel everywhere by car and asked for one of
her own. When Bertie refused, she borrowed one from a friend.
Finally Bertie gave way and she bought a Wolseley.

As monarch, Bertie wanted to do everything. He would open
all his own letters, he insisted. But there were some four hundred
a day and this self-imposed task was clearly impossible. He
would personally sign all military and naval commissions, he
said. But again there were too many.

But what he could do, he did. He worked hard and he played
as hard as ever. Overweight as he was, he quickly became more
and more exhausted.

On 14th June 1902, with Alix, Georgie (now Prince of Wales)
and Toria, he journeyed to Aldershot for the coronation tattoo.
That night, shivery and in pain, he was unable to keep a dinner
appointment. Next day, while a carriage took him to Windsor,
Georgie and Alix reviewed the troops in his place. Bertie was too
ill to make his usual visit to Ascot, though Alix went. He had
lumbago, it was announced. In fact, he had appendicitis, at a time
when appendectomy was still in its infancy.

The coronation had been fixed for 26th June and London was
already packed with royalties from Europe, Russia, China, Japan,
Siam, Ethiopia, Zanzibar, Egypt and Korea. Peritonitis set in and
Bertie's condition became rapidly worse. His physicians advised
surgery but he would not have it.

"After the coronation, you may cut me in two if you like," he
told them, "but I can't disappoint the people."

On 23rd June, a close, muggy day, he returned to London.
Feverish and in pain, he slumped in his seat, his eyes closed, as his
carriage, with its mounted escort clattered from Paddington
station to the palace. Alix, beside him, tried not to show how
tense and worried she felt. As the London crowd roared its
welcome, she bowed and waved in return as though nothing
was wrong. She touched Bertie as a reminder for him to do

likewise. He opened his eyes, but the struggle to raise his hand to his hat was almost too much for him.

There was a dinner party at the palace that night. Bertie wanted to go, but Alix would not permit it and he was now too ill to argue with her. He allowed himself to be put to bed and given a sleeping draught.

Tense with anxiety, Alix dressed and attended the dinner, doing her best to smile at the guests as though nothing was wrong. No one mentioned Bertie's absence. But everyone noticed, of course.

More than anything Alix wanted to be with Bertie. But she could not—must not—leave her guests. It was after midnight when she was finally free to rush back to his side.

Surgery now was imperative, the physicians told her. Without it, Bertie would die an uncrowned King.

A room was hurriedly prepared for the operation. Early next morning Bertie was taken into it. Alix went with him, watching as the anaesthetic was administered, moving impulsively forward to help hold him as he began to struggle. Only with difficulty could she be prevailed to leave the room and wait in the adjoining bedroom. Forty minutes later, Sir Frederick Treves of the London Hospital and Lister, the "father" of antiseptic surgery, came through to tell her that the operation had been a complete success.

Outside the palace, workmen, knowing nothing of the drama inside, were still erecting stands for the coronation. Bertie, coming round from the anaesthetic, complained about the noise of hammering.

He made a surprisingly rapid recovery—the day after the operation he was already sitting up in bed smoking cigars—but there could, of course, be no coronation on 26th June. It was postponed until 9th August. Only unavoidable commitments, like receiving some of the foreign dignitaries who had come to attend the coronation, could take Alix from her husband's bedside. Her place was with him, she said, and there she stayed.

Three weeks after the operation they left the palace in secret. Bertie was carried in a special chair to where a specially adapted vehicle, a cross between a bus and an ambulance, was waiting. The windows were curtained as they drove through the streets of London on their way to Portsmouth. Alix, peeping out surreptitiously, wondered what people would think if they knew who was in the vehicle.

Bertie, good though his recovery had been, was not yet ready to face the people. First there was to be a convalescent cruise on the *Victoria and Albert*. As the yacht steamed south, he lay on the deck in the sun, a process which quickly bored him. He tried to pass the time reading, but that was something else which quickly palled. He had never been a book-man. He filled in much of his time writing letters in an impatient, sometimes almost illegible hand. More than anything else, he needed people to talk to. Alix was with him, but to talk to her meant shouting and that tired him. Failing her, he talked to anyone who chanced to be handy. Even a passing sailor would be hailed and dragged into hesitant, respectful conversation.

Bored though he may have been, Bertie benefitted from the cruise. His illness and the diet his doctors had advised reduced his weight by nearly thirty pounds. His waist measurement was down from 44 inches to 36 inches, and that, Alix felt, was good.

It was a bronzed and fit-looking Bertie, noticeably less irritable, who was crowned in Westminster Abbey on 9th August, the customary four-hour ceremony having been cut to two-and-a-half hours to avoid fatiguing him. Alix was as unpunctual as ever. She took so long dressing for the occasion that Bertie went so far as to burst in upon her.

"If you don't come immediately you won't be crowned Queen," he threatened, half-jokingly.

He was in excellent humour. In the Grand Hall of the palace, where their grandchildren were waiting to see them leave, he did an impromptu jig in his purple robe.

"There's funny old Grandpa for you," he chortled.

Inside the abbey, some of Bertie's feminine favourites, among them Alice Keppel, Sarah Bernhardt, Jennie Churchill, Princess Daisy of Pless and Mrs Arthur Paget, were privileged to watch the ceremony from a special box. "The King's Loose Box", it was sniggeringly nicknamed. But Alix, in a dress of gold gauze, her crimson train lined with miniver, trimmed with ermine and embroidered in gold, outshone them all. At fifty-seven, she looked both youthful and radiant still.

Georgie, as Prince of Wales, was the first to pay homage to the newly-crowned King. Impulsively, Bertie clutched him and kissed him on both cheeks. Alix, watching, felt tears prick her eyes.

Moving though the incident was, for her it was not the most inspiring moment of the whole ceremony. That was the anointing. So moved was she that, returning to the palace, she would not permit the smear of holy oil to be wiped from her forehead.

For Bertie, perhaps the most moving moment came when Alix was crowned Queen—as the assembled peeresses, at the same moment, all raised their coronets from their laps and placed them upon their heads. This simultaneous movement of white-gloved arms framing dark heads, he felt was "like a scene from a beautiful ballet".

THE SWINGING SEASON

By the season of 1903 it was no longer necessary to mourn for Queen Victoria. For Bertie and Alix, it was a swinging season, quite like the early days of marriage. They entertained lavishly and Buckingham Palace, which had been so little used in the years since Albert's death, now became the focal point of both monarchy and aristocratic pleasure. Gay receptions at night took the place of the old dull, dreary afternoon Drawing Rooms. During Ascot week Bertie gave a ball for 900 guests in the windowless Waterloo Chamber at Windsor, the first state ball held at Windsor for sixty years.

If monarchy had created a new, less easy-going Alix, Bertie was still the same old Bertie. It was quickly clear that he was not going to allow his new role as King to interfere with his personal way of life. He still visited Alice in Portman Square and Agnes in Grosvenor Cresent; still spent weekends with his friends at their country homes. With or without Alix, he travelled as much as ever—to Sandringham and Balmoral; Cowes, Ascot, Epsom, Goodwood; to Paris and Biarritz, where his hotel wing had its own private dining room overlooking the sea. Caesar, his fox terrier, went everywhere with him.

"Papa is always so much away now from home," Alix wrote sadly to Georgie.

In Paris and Biarritz, Bertie would meet up with Alice Keppel She might travel independently, but everyone knew she was the

King's mistress and treated her with the deference due to a royal personage. Often she had her two small daughters along. They knew Bertie as "Kingy".

Alice was at Chatsworth too when Bertie and Alix went there each January to stay with Lottie, now in her seventies but still battling to retain a vestige of her former beauty.

Each spring Bertie and Alix took a cruise aboard the *Victoria and Albert* with thirty servants and a crew of 300. For Alix, the cruise was equivalent to moving house. She insisted on taking along all her favourite knick-knacks so that her white and gold cabin, with its grand piano, was every bit as cluttered as her apartment at the palace. For his part, Bertie had a special cabin to hold his wardrobe of suits and uniforms.

As King, he was fussier than ever about clothes—his own and others. The wrong buttons on a uniform, decorations worn in the wrong order, a bowler worn instead of a topper, too long a train to a dress—and he was quick to reprimand the guilty party.

"This is a dinner party, not a tennis supper," he corrected one young lady who so far forgot herself as to turn up displaying an inch or two of ankle.

Marienbad became a new port of call in his crowded travel itinerary. He went there without Alix, ostensibly to take the waters. Sixty-five pieces of luggage holding forty suits and twenty pairs of shoes went with him. Fresh-faced and again overweight at 224 pounds, he rose regularly at eight o'clock in his first-floor suite at the Hotel Weimar, dressed as immaculately as always and set out on a pre-breakfast stroll. His reputation as a womanizer preceded him, with the result that many elegant ladies found themselves up and about equally early, many of them dressed in gowns more suited to an evening ball than a morning stroll.

He played croquet and bridge, and disliked being beaten at either. On the rare occasions when he did lose at bridge he met his losses from the big roll of banknotes he always carried in his pockets. He had given up golf; practice at Sandringham had not made him sufficiently proficient. He took the waters and was supposed to be on a diet, but lunch and dinner, though relatively plain, were always substantial. On Sundays he went to the Anglican church.

Once or twice, on these visits to Marienbad, he ran into an old flame, Lillie Langtry, white-haired now. Bertie's taste, as always, was for younger women, like the attractive fraulein who sold Styrian hats in a shop on the Kirchenplatz. He was often in the shop and made purchases from time to time on condition that she delivered them to him personally at his hotel. Staying with Lottie at Chatsworth one year, he attempted a pursuit of the blonde and beautiful Princess Daisy of Pless (the former Daisy Cornwallis-West). When she declined to be "nice" to him, he called her "a humbug".

Bertie was eating too much, smoking too much, working too hard, playing too hard. Occasionally he had what seemed like fainting fits. Alix worried about him, but neither she nor his doctors could persuade him to take things more easily. He would rather risk his health than be bored. He developed chronic bronchitis and by 1905—the year their son-in-law, Charles, became Haakon VII of Norway—this had become so bad that Alix was really concerned. She had been to Portugal on an official visit and planned to go on to Denmark to see her father. Instead, she persuaded Bertie to meet her in Marseilles for a Mediterranean cruise she hoped would benefit him. But three weeks of shipboard life was enough for Bertie. Leaving Alix to visit Greece on her own, he quit the yacht and headed for Paris.

That autumn Georgie and May set off on a tour of India, again leaving the children in Alix's grandmotherly care. As usual she spoiled them. There were now six of them, including George, born in 1902, and John, a baby of four months who was to develop epilepsy and die in his sleep at the age of thirteen. But that, mercifully, was hidden in the future as Alix, thoroughly enjoying her role of grandmother, bathed him at bedtime, taught the other children to paint, read them stories and watched the two elder boys attend their first hunt. With Bertie living his own life and Georgie again away, the grandchildren helped to fill a big gap in her life. Her charity work also helped. She organized a fund to help "the poor, starving unemployed" and started it off with a donation of £2000. Within months it had soared to £150,000.

In January 1906, word reached Alix that her father had died in Copenhagen at the age of eighty-eight. She was deeply upset; sorry she could not have been with him, but glad that Minnie had been there. To cheer her up, Bertie took her to Paris. They travelled incognito and stayed at the British Embassy, giving a number of small luncheon and dinner parties.

With the death of their father, Alix and Minnie, close though they had always been, were drawn yet closer . . . to each other and to their native Denmark. They would still meet in Denmark whenever possible, they decided. They found themselves a large cottage close to the seashore at Hvidore and set about converting it into a holiday home. The work of conversion was not yet complete when Alix took Bertie to see it. The billiards room was going to be turned into a guest room, she explained to him, adding the hope that he would occupy it from time to time. He never did.

He was troubled around this time by an ulcer on the side of his nose. It was feared at first that it might be malignant. But radium treatment cleared it.★ Relieved and impressed by this new wonder of medical science, Bertie persuaded Cassel and another friend, Lord Iveagh, to found the Radium Institute in London similar to the one already in existence in Paris.

That spring Minnie came to England to stay with Alix. Together, the two sisters visited hospitals and orphanages, theatres and art galleries, went shopping and sightseeing. As always, they were completely happy in each other's company. So much so that Minnie repeated her visit the following year.

A less welcome visitor was nephew Willy in the company of his wife, the tall, tight-waisted Kaiserin. Bertie took him out shooting and arranged a command performance in his honour. But uncle and nephew still disliked each other as much as ever and Willy's snide comments about Alice Keppel did nothing to improve the relationship.

More enjoyable was the visit Bertie and Alix paid to Nicky and Alicky in the summer of 1908. Because of unrest in Russia, it was thought too dangerous for them all to meet on land. Instead, they arranged a rendezvous in the Baltic. For Alix and Bertie, it meant a rough crossing. A gale was raging in the North Sea and

---

★ There is in the library of the Royal College of Surgeons a manuscript by Sir Frederick Treves dealing with this and other aspects of Bertie's health during his years of monarchy. Unfortunately, our request to be permitted to consult it was refused. "It is not the Queen's custom," we were informed by Buckingham Palace, "to allow confidential information about the health of her family, living or dead, to be released."

the *Victoria and Albert* was so pitched and tossed that much of Alix's precious bric-à-brac, without which she never travelled, was smashed to smithereens and many of the party were seasick, though Alix was not. The rougher it was, the more she seemed to thrive on it. Fog shrouded the Baltic where Nicky and Alicky awaited them aboard the *Standart* and the *Polar Star*. With them, to make it as much a family as a state occasion, were their children and Nicky's mother, Minnie, whose presence raised a delicate question of protocol when the Russian party boarded the *Victoria and Albert* for dinner. Who took precedence, Minnie as Dowager Empress or her daughter-in-law, Alicky, the Empress? Bertie solved the problem in his jovial fashion by taking one on each arm and leading them into dinner together.

The Olympic Games were held in London that year and Alix was at the White City the day they ran the Marathon. Like everyone else, she was caught up in the emotion of the moment, thumping the floor with her umbrella as Dorando Pietri, the Italian, first man back in the stadium, swayed and staggered his exhausted way round the track.

With the finishing tape only yards away, fellow-Italians caught Pietri as he fell, holding him and pushing him across the line just ahead of Hayes, the American.

Frantic confusion followed and the crowd roared its disapproval as the judges decided that Hayes had won (Pietri had been helped).

Alix restored the situation by announcing that she would give the Italian a special cup. She had it inscribed "For Dorando Pietri in remembrance of the marathon race from Windsor to the Stadium from Queen Alexandra" and was at the White City again on the last day of the Games to present it personally.

She might feel for others, but nobody thought of her. More and more she felt neglected, lonely, unwanted. An attack of influenza that winter left her depressed. Neuralgia plagued her, too. More than ever she was worried about Bertie. He seemed always tired, sometimes depressed, often touchy. Both were far from well that February of 1909—a year in which Bertie (with Minoru) was again to win the Derby amidst scenes of wild emotion—when they set off on a state visit to Willy in Berlin. Willy, as always, did everything he could to impress Uncle Bertie. Twenty thousand troops lined the route as Bertie and

Alix drove from the station to Willy's place. But the programme his nephew had arranged was to prove too exhausting for the uncle. Bertie's bronchitis was again troublesome and endless big cigars did nothing to help the resulting cough.

He was sitting on a sofa with Daisy of Pless after luncheon at the British Embassy, smoking yet another cigar, when a fit of coughing seized him. He coughed until he fell, exhausted, against the back of the sofa. His cigar dropped from his fingers, his face was deathly white and his protuberant eyes bulged more than ever. Daisy, as she fumbled with the collar of his uniform, trying to loosen it, thought he was dying. Alix ran over and tried also to loosen his collar. Neither of them succeeded. The room was cleared and a doctor was summoned. Bertie himself finally managed to unfasten his collar and presently the coughing stopped.

That evening he attended the state ball which Willy had arranged, but did not dance. The following evening, tired after a drive to Potsdam and lunch with the 1st Prussian Dragoon Guards, he attended a gala performance of *Sardanapalus* at the Opera House. So exhausted was he that he fell asleep in his seat. He awoke with a start during the final scene—the funeral pyre of Sardanapalus—to find, as he thought, the Opera House on fire. Only with some difficulty could Willy's wife, sitting beside him, convince him that the fire was staged and under control and that there was no danger.

"THEY TOOK HIM AWAY FROM ME"

On 6th March 1910, Bertie left London for his customary stay in Biarritz with Alice Keppel. By chance, a day or so before leaving he ran into one of his old flames, darling Daisy. He was looking ill and depressed, she thought—"greatly changed".

He journeyed to Biarritz by way of Paris, where he stayed, as usual, at the Hotel Bristol. But he was no longer the same gay Bertie who had once made Paris his favourite stamping ground. Bronchitis troubled him, he was suffering from the after-effects of an injection against influenza and was plagued by rheumatism. At night he slept with a string of sherry corks twined round each leg. Someone had told him it was good for rheumatism.

More than anything, he was beginning to feel his age. All the same, he sent for Willy Clarkson, the make-up expert, to touch up the greyness of his beard and went to the Porte St Martin theatre to see Rostand's *Chanteclair*. The theatre was draughty and a bronchial chill, similar to the one he had had in Berlin, quickly developed. When he reached Biarritz he collapsed.

Alix, when she heard, was torn between wifely duty and her constant dread of public humiliation. Much as she wanted to be with Bertie at this time, she was put off by the knowledge that Alice Keppel was already with him. Wife and mistress could hardly sit together by the sick King's bedside.

Her conflict was resolved by fresh news from Biarritz. Bertie was much improved. She had already planned a Mediterranean cruise aboard their new yacht, *Alexandra* and she wrote urging Bertie to join her.

Quite impossible, he informed her. He assured her that there was no longer anything to worry about and pressed her to undertake the cruise on her own. So Alix sailed for Corfu.

From Biarritz, where he was occupying the ground floor of the hotel because stairs meant too much exertion for him, Bertie wrote to Lady Paget: "I am all right again and am enjoying my stay." But to those around him he looked far from well and desperately old all at once. Gone was the old *joie-de-vivre*, as he perhaps sensed himself. And it was perhaps a presentiment of the future which caused him to remark, "I shall be sorry to leave Biarritz—perhaps for good."

He returned to London on 27th April. Georgie met him at Victoria station. Far from well though he was, Bertie still could not bring himself to take life quietly. He had to be out and about, doing something, fighting off boredom. He went to a private view at the Royal Academy and, with Georgie and May, to the opera at Covent Garden. On Friday Georgie brought his two eldest sons, David, now fifteen, and Bertie, fourteen, to have lunch with their grandfather at the palace.

Bertie spent the weekend at his beloved Sandringham. On Saturday, in a biting wind, he was pottering about the gardens with the head gardener. On Sunday he went to church. But he felt too tired to walk across the park, as usual, and went instead in his carriage. After lunch, in wet, blustery weather, he was again wandering about the estate.

By the time he returned to London on Monday another chill had developed. Despite it, he went round that evening to have dinner with Agnes Keyser. She saw he was far from well and insisted that he leave early.

He awoke the following morning wheezing for breath. His doctors were called and diagnosed his old trouble—bronchitis. They advised him to rest. But Bertie could no more rest than pigs can fly. For him, it was business as usual. Among the people he saw that day was Whitelaw Reid, the U.S. ambassador. They discussed arrangements for the following week's visit of ex-President Teddy Roosevelt and Bertie accepted an invitation to dine with him at Dorchester House. But Reid, who had suffered from bronchial asthma himself, wondered if the King was not worse than his vigorous and energetic nature would admit.

Alix, on her way back from Corfu, was now in Venice. She planned to stay there several days. But when a telegram reached her informing her of Bertie's condition, she packed immediately and set off for home. Not that she was unduly alarmed. Bertie had had these chills and coughs before . . . in Berlin, in Biarritz. But now that Alice was out of the way, she wanted to be with him.

She reached Calais to find a letter from Georgie awaiting her. Papa's cough was troublesome, he wrote, and he was sleeping badly. Both he and May were very worried.

For the first time, Alix began to feel frightened.

She crossed the Channel in the teeth of a gale. Georgie and May were waiting to greet her when her train pulled in at Victoria Station. With them, she hurried to Buckingham Palace. It was 5th May.

She found Bertie up and dressed, sitting in his favourite chair. His face was drained of colour, a ghastly grey, and he had difficulty in breathing.

He had reserved a box for her that evening at Covent Garden, he told her, coughing. It was a performance of *Siegfried*. She would enjoy it. But Alix, now that she was with him, had no intention of leaving him again.

"I have come to be with you," she said.

The next day—Friday—Bertie was expecting Lord Knollys and Ernest Cassel. Ill though he was, he insisted, despite protests from those around him, on getting up and dressing as formally and immaculately as always. He sat again in his favourite chair, but rose to shake hands with Cassel.

"I am very seedy," he said, his voice more guttural and less distinct than usual, "but I wanted to see you."

For a few minutes the two men chatted briefly. When Cassel left Bertie had a light lunch. After it, as always, he lighted one of his big cigars. Then he collapsed.

Nurses helped him into his favourite chair and Toria flew in search of Mama. By the time Alix got to him Bertie had had the first of a series of heart attacks.

Warned by that unseen chord which binds husband and wife, Alix knew somehow that Bertie was dying. There were now five doctors in attendance, but there was, she knew instinctively, nothing they could do.

It was then that Alix performed what was perhaps the most unselfish act of her whole married life. The dead Vicky, writing to the dead Queen Victoria, had once praised her high sense of duty. Never, in her loyalty to and love for Bertie, was it higher than now. She sent for Alice, his mistress.

Alice came. At forty-one, she was plump and matronly now rather than vivacious and voluptuous as she had once been. Alix took her to Bertie's bedroom. Dying though he was, drifting at times into unconsciousness, he was still in his formal clothes, still sitting in his armchair, obstinately refusing to take to his bed.

"I shall not give in. I shall go on. I shall work to the end," he insisted.

Georgie came in with the news that Bertie's horse, Witch of the Air, had won the Spring Plate for two-year-olds at Kempton Park by half-a-length.

"Yes, I heard," his father whispered in reply. "I am very glad."

Alice left and Alix again took her rightful place as wife beside her dying husband. As the evening shadows lengthened outside in the palace gardens, Bertie again drifted into unconsciousness. He was beyond protest when Alix had him lifted out of his chair, carried to the bed and undressed. Loving him more than ever in his moments of dying, she sat at the bedside.

Georgie and May, Louise and Toria joined her. Just before midnight, as the doctors attempted to revive him with oxygen, Bertie died.

Alix felt—her own words—as if "I have been turned to stone". From her, as yet, there were no tears. "I am unable to cry, unable to grasp the meaning of it all, incapable of doing anything."

Bertie, with all his faults, had been the love of her life. In life, she had been forced to share him with so many other women. But now, in death, she finally had her beloved, erring, erratic Bertie all to herself. She wanted to keep it that way—to keep him with her. It was eleven days before she could be persuaded to surrender the body for its lying-in-state in Westminster Hall.

It was then that she broke down and cried.

"They took him away from me," she said, piteously, "What will become of me?"

POSTSCRIPT

Alix was sixty-five when Bertie died, still elegantly beautiful, still looking much younger than her years. But now, as though the light had somehow gone out of her life, she was to age with increasing rapidity. Yet two things about her—her hands and her eyes—were to remain beautiful to the end.

In a message she wrote herself, she thanked Britain and the world for its sympathy in her bereavement "from the depths of my poor broken heart". She was less grateful to Parliament for the fact that it made her widow's annuity subject to tax, a move which had the effect of halving her income. Despite the comparative poverty of her early upbringing, she had never had a head for money and now, in widowhood, she continued to live as extravagantly as ever, spending freely, giving generously to charity.

With Bertie's death, his dog, Caesar, became her favourite pet and constant companion. But in other outward respects she did not live solely with Bertie's memory as her mother-in-law, Queen Victoria, had lived with Albert's ghost. Dutiful as she had always been in both her personal and public lives, she continued to support her favourite charities, and visit hospitals. With the institution of Alexandra Rose Day in 1913 to mark the fiftieth anniversary of her arrival in England to marry Bertie, she began a practice of driving through London in her barouche to encourage people to give freely. She dreaded the painful memories each fresh Rose Day brought her, but she did it just the same.

Muddled and unpunctual as she had always been, it took her months to organize the move back to Marlborough House following Bertie's death and it was nearly Christmas when Georgie and May, as the new King and Queen, finally took over at the palace. Her sister, Minnie, who had rushed to her side just as Alix had gone to Russia when Sasha died, helped her with the move. At Sandringham she continued to occupy the 'Big House' which Bertie had bequeathed to her as part of his personal estate while Georgie and May and their children contented themselves with the more cramped confines of York Cottage. Her un-married daughter, Toria, was her almost constant, if increasingly bitter and frustrated, companion.

To Alix, in her early years of widowhood, it must have seemed that death was all around her. Old friends and relatives were dying off: Lady Macclesfield, who had helped to bring dear, dead Eddy into the world; Louise's husband, Macduff; Alix's brother, Freddy, King of Denmark.

She was shocked to learn that her other brother, Willy, King of Greece, had been assassinated in the streets of Salonika. Yet more terrible was the news that her namesake, Alicky, together with her husband, Nicky, and their children had been brutally massacred in a cellar at Ekaterinburg.

Shattered and depressed, no longer able to face the public, no longer wanting to live in London, no longer well enough to travel to Hvidore, the holiday home she shared with Minnie in Denmark, she retired almost completely to Sandringham. Almost totally deaf now, complaining often of pain and noises in her head, crippled and bronchial, she walked in the park or by -the neighbouring seashore, drove round the estate in her carriage and sometimes motored into nearby King's Lynn. Giant jigsaw puzzles preoccupied her of an evening and there was always a reading from the Bible at bedtime. She wrote endlessly to Georgie at Buckingham Palace, letters which were increasingly rambling and less than coherent, and read avidly the letters he dutifully wrote to 'old Motherdear" in return.

Just as she had once worried about a bride for Eddy, so she worried now that Georgie's eldest son, David, Prince of Wales, though well into his twenties, was not yet married. A letter from David's brother, Bertie, the Duke of York, about a visit he had paid to Laeken revived old memories. She wrote back telling him how another Bertie, his grandfather, had once walked with her in the gardens at Laeken, how he had proposed to her and she had accepted.

More and more, as old people will, she found herself looking back down the long corridor of the years, reliving old joys, experiencing afresh old hurts. More and more the past and the present seemed to become one—until on 20th November 1925, following a heart attack, she died in her bedroom at Sandringham, convinced that death was but a gateway to a happy reunion with the husband who, for all his unfaithfulness, she had never ceased to love. A few more days and she would have been eighty-one.

BIBLIOGRAPHY

Letters of Queen Victoria 1837–61, ed. A. C. Benson and Viscount Esher
Letters of Queen Victoria 1862–85 and *1886–1901*, both series ed. G. E. Buckle
Further Letters of Queen Victoria, ed. Hector Bolitho
Dearest Child, Dearest Mama and *Your Dear Letter* (letters between Queen Victoria and the Crown Princess of Prussia), all three ed. Roger Fulford
Personal Letters of King Edward VII, ed. Lieut. Col. J. P. C. Sewell
King Edward VII, Sir Philip Magnus
King Edward VII, E. F. Benson
King Edward VII, Sir Sidney Lee
King Edward and His Times, Andre Maurois
The Private Life of Edward VII, one of His Majesty's Servants
The Life and Times of Edward VII, Keith Middlemass
The Tragedy of Edward VII, W. H. Edwards
King Edward VII in his True Colours, Edward Legge
King Edward VII as a Sportsman, A. E. T. Watson
Edward VII and his Circle, Virginia Cowles
Edward VII at Marienbad, Sigmund Munz
Concerning Queen Victoria and Her Son, Sir George Arthur
Victoria's Heir, George Dangerfield
Edward VII and Alexandra, H. and A. Gernsheim
Queen Alexandra, Sir George Arthur
Queen Alexandra, Georgina Battiscombe
The Private Life of Queen Alexandra, Hans Madol
Unpredictable Queen, E. E. P. Tisdall
Victoria, R. I., Elizabeth Longford
Sixty Years A Queen, Sir Herbert Maxwell
King George V, Arthur Bryant

King George V, Harold Nicolson
King George V, John Gore
Queen Mary, J. Pope Hennessy
Queen Mary, Sir George Arthur
Prince and Princess of Wales, Anon.
For My Grandchildren, H.R.H. Princess Alice
Nicholas and Alexandra, Robert K. Massie
Daisy, Princess of Pless, by Herself
From My Private Diary, Daisy Princess of Pless
Embassies of Other Days, Walburga Lady Paget
Scenes and Memories, Walburga Lady Paget
The Reminiscences of Lady Randolph Churchill
Lady Randolph Churchill, 1854–95, Ralph G. Martin
Darling Daisy, Theo Lang
Skittles (The Life and Times of Catherine Walters), Henry Blyth
The Girl With the Swansdown Sea, Cyril Pearl
The Pearl From Plymouth, W. H. Holden
The Days I Knew, Lillie Langtry
The Gilded Lily, Ernest Dudley
Life's Ebb and Flow, Frances Countess of Warwick
Edwardian Daughter, Sonia Keppel
Edwardian Hey-Days, G. F. M. Cornwallis-West
Ma Double Vie, Sarah Bernhardt
Sarah Bernhardt, Lysiane Bernhardt
Sarah the Divine, Arthur William Rowe
Madame Sarah, Cornelius Otis Skinner
The Private Life of Mr Gladstone, Richard Deacon
Royal Homes, Neville Williams
The Royal Palaces, Philip Howard
Marlborough House, Arthur H. Beavan
Sandringham Past and Present, Mrs Herbert Jones
18 Years on the Sandringham Estate, Mrs Gerald Cresswell
Sandringham, Helen Cathcart
The Court at Windsor, Christopher Hibbert
Mordaunt v. Mordaunt, Anon.
The Baccarat Case, ed. W. Teignmouth Shore
Cheating at Cards, John Welcome
The Courtesans, Joanna Richardson
The Mistresses, Betty Kelen

Gilded Beauties of the Second Empire, Frederick Loliée (adapted by
   Bryan O'Donnell)
The Age of Optimism, James Laver
Roads to Ruin, E. S. Turner
The Worm in the Bud, Ronald Pearsall

INDEX